Originally from India, Satyam Sikha Moorty received his PhD in American Literature from the University of Utah, Salt Lake City, and taught for 31 years at Southern Utah University, Cedar City, Utah, courses such as F. Scott Fitzgerald, Shakespeare, Eastern Literatures in English translation (Indian, Chinese, and Japanese); was a Fulbright professor in Yemen, Moldova, (thrice), Austria, and Azerbaijan; was a Balkan scholar at the American University in Bulgaria; published scholarly articles in the U.S., India, France, Spain, Romania, Moldova, Azerbaijan, and Ukraine; published poetry in the U.S., India, Canada, the U.K., South Africa, Moldova, and Azerbaijan; published a book of poems and short stories titled Distant Lands, Diverse Cultures and Moldova: Vigorous Heritage and Variegated Traditions: Poems, Essays, Stories, and Speeches.

Family	Surviving brother	V.K.N. Murthy Sikha
	Son	Naresh Sikha
	Daughter-in-law	Anna (Annapoorna Malyala) Sikha
	Grandson	Ishwar Satyanand Sikha
	Daughter	Neela Moorty Mummaneni
	Son-in-law	Bobby Mummaneni
	Granddaughter	Priya Mummaneni
	Grandson	Jay Ramprasad Mummaneni
	Friends	Jim and Terri Cotts Jim Aton and Carrie Trenholm Roger Anderson and Sandy Gillies Ed McNicoll Eric Morrow
	Mentors	The late Dr. Jack Adamson The late Dr. William Mulder

My students

and Lakshmi Sikha Moorty

Satyam Sikha Moorty

PASSAGE FROM INDIA: ESSAYS, POEMS, AND STORIES

AUSTIN MACAULEY PUBLISHERS™

LONDON • CAMBRIDGE • NEW YORK • SHARJAH

A CIP catalogue record for this title is available from the British Library.

ISBN 9781528927239 (Paperback)
ISBN 9781528964999 (ePub e-book)

www.austinmacauley.com

First Published (2019)
Austin Macauley Publishers Ltd
25 Canada Square
Canary Wharf
London
E14 5LQ

Most of the poems in their original versions appeared in: *Weber Studies, Dialogue, Dialogue and Alliance, Tailwind, The Poet's Page,* Café Bellas Artes, *Panorama, Encyclia, South Asia Quarterly International*, Distinguished Faculty Honor Lecture Committee, Southern Utah University, *Hinduism Today, Etudes, Earthshine, Utah Sings, Sand and Sky; an anthology* (Rumi Poetry Club), *Mind Magazine, Telugu Paluku* (TANA souvenir issues), *Telugu Sahiti Sampada* (souvenir issue U.S.A.), *Asian-American Writing, The Journal of Indian Writing in English, Taj Mahal Review, Kritya, Muse India, Cyber Wit (India); Indian Voices – an anthology (Canada), Rangoli (U.K.); Tonight, An Anthology of World Love Poetry (South Africa), Middle East Times* (Yemen), *Sofia Echo* (Bulgaria), American Studies Center of Moldova's Annual Conference publications. Some of the previously published poems have been slightly revised with 'notes' appended for the present collection.

Table of Contents

Stories 175

Essays

Can One Be Spiritual Without Being a Ritualist?

Rituals by nature tend to be outward, celebratory, social, and congregation oriented, while spiritualism is inward-looking and individual-oriented like 'atman'. Rituals impose limitations, while spiritualism liberates an individual.

Social rituals up to a point are in order to promote social cohesion, whereas religious rituals practiced blindly and indiscriminately tend to dilute spirituality. All religious and social rituals are man-made which tend to restrict man's independent thinking. On the other hand, spiritualism is individual-oriented that promotes solace and spiritual fulfillment. When an individual experiences hollowness and emptiness within himself, he needs to transport himself inward to overcome such emptiness and commune with the Maker/God. No one can guide the individual toward salvation except a one-on-one consultation with a 'guru' or a prayer without the fanfare of ritualism.

To seek spiritualism, one doesn't have to go after human company; in fact, spiritualism thrives on solitude. Solitude doesn't imply loneliness or being alone. Yes, one can be spiritual without being a ritualist. By the same token, if one is morally and ethically pure, then where is the need for religion? Then what is the purpose of religion? The eighteenth-century writer and philosopher Voltaire pointed out that if there is no God, create one. Surely, then, religion is not for ethical or moral needs which are actually man-made but for the higher needs of man—spiritualism. The famous nineteenth-century American Transcendentalist Henry David Thoreau removed himself from metropolitan Boston,

Massachusetts, to a small, uninhabited wooded Walden Pond to 'simplify' his life and to be immersed in spiritualism. So did several Hindu sages and swamis.

This greatly explains the Hindu 'sanyasa' stage.

But the city-dwellers don't have to sacrifice their essential material needs and comforts and their social involvement to seek spiritualism. Being a ritualist, on the other hand, prompts an individual to seek a congregation or to make a trip to a temple or a church in order to belong to the ostentatious ritualist-oriented performances.

In my own daily life, living in a small American university town without a Hindu temple, I am able to feel comfortable spiritually without feeling discarded or disowned by my faith. I live by my faith in my small abode. I never feel lonely. I don't perform rituals, yet I believe in God and pray to Him continually. I am responsible to myself with belief in God as my guiding principle. "Words without thoughts never to heaven go." (*Hamlet*, Act III, Scene iii, 98). I don't want to be caught in the intricate web of religious rituals. I may practice them minimally on occasion. Yet I don't mean to deny the need for rituals in social and cultural matters or when I visit a temple in a major metropolis. We are all social beings.

> My God! He hasn't bestowed on me riches;
> yet His immanence nourishes my being,
> to face the world compressed by
> terror, fear, hatred, and prejudice.

(The last stanza of my poem "Lines Composed upon Reading a Line—God, ever-present divine principle is always with us.")

Mahatma Gandhi and the American Imagination

Since December 1982 when Sir Richard Attenborough's *Gandhi* was screened in the major cities of America and around the world, Mahatma Gandhi, one of the outstanding personalities not only of our time but of all times, who revealed to all a power not of rifles and guns, but the power innate in each individual, a power which this war-haunted world can exploit fully in making wars impossible, has once again become a significant part of world consciousness, subject for anecdotes about his work and life in newspapers, magazines, TV, radio, and conversation; older citizens have begun reminiscing about the interest that Gandhi had generated when they were young. In fact, as recently as February 23, 1984, a reader of *The Salt Lake Tribune* in his letter to the editor reminds the readers of the newspaper that:

We could profit by refreshing our recollections of the thoughts and the teachings of Gandhi. Responding to violence with violence, even though brave, is the law of the lower nature. It continues to beget more violence, which in turn responds with more violence, in a never-ending cycle.

But responding with non-violence is the law of the higher nature, and it requires a restraint of passions involving a higher form of courage. It is the only means for mankind to free itself from the barbarism of violence against violence and enter the higher realm of nobility of the spirit in which all men are brothers. Then they can unite in attacking the common enemies of mankind: poverty, pestilence, disease, ignorance, and crime.

Is it too much to hope that there will emerge leaders in the world who have the wisdom to see the rightness and the righteousness of those views and who have the acumen and the courage to give them a try? Sadly, it is not likely in our time, but hopefully, maybe for our children, or for our grandchildren, if this race shall last that long.

As the personality of Gandhi recedes from us physically and in time, the outlines of his urgent message to humanity, as the writer to the *Tribune* so eloquently testifies, seem to become clearer and sharper than before.

Gandhism is not simply a theory to be expounded for quibbling or tautological debate, not merely an abstract idea for intellectual gymnastics, but something that ought to be the core of our normal thinking and activity.

For Gandhi was essentially a man of action, a 'karmayogi', who assigned 'overriding priority to practical work over sermons', who practiced what he preached, who backed his precepts with practical measures. In his own words, "What I have done will endure, not what I have said and written." In a comment on the *Gita,* the Hindu philosophical document, the Song of God, Gandhi defined the perfect karma yogi:

He is a devotee who is jealous of none, who is a fount of mercy, who is without egotism, who is selfless, who treats alike cold and heat, happiness and misery, who is ever forgiving, who is always contented, whose resolutions are firm, who has dedicated mind and soul to God, who causes no dread, who is not afraid of others, who is free from exultation, sorrow and fear, who is pure, who is versed in action yet remains unaffected by it, who renounces all fruit, good or bad, who treats friend and foe alike, who is untouched by respect or disrespect, who is not puffed up by praise, who does not go under when people speak ill of him, who loves silence and solitude, and who has a disciplined reason. Such devotion is inconsistent with the existence at the same time of strong attachments.[1]

This saint-like benefactor, although born into a well-to-do Hindu family and educated in law at the University of London, gave up a flourishing law practice to devote himself wholeheartedly and single-mindedly to lead a nonviolent crusade in freeing his people from British oppression. Affluence he discarded voluntarily and subjected himself to a life of poverty to identify himself in all respects with the masses of his native country. Self-controlled, self-motivated, and self-directed, Gandhi pursued a truth-oriented, love-directed, and conscience-guided life exerting a mighty fight against racial prejudice and discrimination and inequality of man. The most notable experience that Mahatma Gandhi recounts in his autobiography, appropriately entitled *The Story of My Experiments with Truth,* a revealing study of the human soul that is both utterly frank and disarmingly honest, which changed the course of his life, is quoted by Hon. Jan H. Hofmeyer, Chancellor of Witwatersrand University, in his essay, 'Gandhi in South Africa'.

...That fell to my lot seven days after I had arrived in South Africa. I had gone there on a purely mundane and selfish mission. I was just a boy returned from England, wanting to make some money. Suddenly the client who had taken me there asked me to go to Pretoria from Durban. It was not an easy journey. There was the railway journey as far as Charlestown and the coach to Johannesburg. On the train, I had a first class ticket, but not a bed ticket. At Maritzburg, when the beds were issued, the guard came and turned me out, and asked me to go into the van compartment. I would not go, and the train steamed away, leaving me shivering in the cold. Now the creative experience comes there. I was afraid for my very life. I entered the dark waiting room. There was a white man in the room. I was afraid of him. 'What was my duty?' I

---

[1] As quoted in Louis Fisher's *Gandhi-His Life and Message for the World* (New York: New American Library, 1954), p. 18.

asked myself. 'Should I go back to India, or should I go forward, with God as my helper, and face whatever was in store for me?' I decided to stay and suffer. My active non-violence began from that date.[2]

Gandhi found himself 'plunged into the midst of the injustices and terrors which are rife in a country beset by race prejudice and the recognition of the color lines'.[3] Moreover, he was profoundly disturbed by the suffering he witnessed in Zululand, causing a permanent change in his life, making him resolve to serve humanity with all his soul.

...To this end, within a few months of his return from Zululand, he adopted three principles by which to live: 'brahmacharya' or celibacy, which was an ancient Hindu vow; 'satyagraha', or the force of truth and love, which was his own invention; and 'ahimsa', or nonviolence to all living things... Gandhi came to believe that his three principles required him to give up everything he owned, treat all people as part of his family, and contribute whatever he earned to community service.[4]

'Satyagraha' for Gandhi represented the active force of love, faith, and sacrifice because he believed that non-violence brought out the indomitable strength of the inner will. The French philosopher, Romain Rolland, who corresponded with Gandhi between 1920 and 1943, considered Gandhi's first non-violent struggle against brute force and tyranny in South Africa as the ultimate victory of 'heroic personality', and cites the three essential features of

---

[2] *Mahatma Gandhi: Essays and Reflections on his Life and Work.* Presented to him on his Seventieth Birthday, October 2, 1939, ed. by S. Radhakrishnan (Bombay: Jaico Publishing House, 1956), pp. 109-110.

[3] John Haynes Holmes, *My Gandhi* (New York: Harper & Brothers, 1953), p. 62.

[4] Ved Mehta, *Mahatma Gandhi and His Apostles* (New York: Penguin Books, 1977), p. 118.

Gandhiji's teachings: moral purity, practicability, and an iron will. For twenty years (1893-1914), South Africa remained Gandhi's home and arena of public service, a testing ground for his ideas; it was in South Africa that he conquered himself, and he conquered the government which oppressed his people. Though essentially imbued with Hindu religious thought, it was in South Africa that Gandhi came under the influence of American, British, and Russian writers in Henry David Thoreau, John Ruskin, and Leo Tolstoy.

The book (Ruskin's *Unto This Last*) was impossible to lay aside, once I had begun it. It gripped me... I determined to change my life in accordance with the ideals of the book.

...I believe that I discovered some of my deepest convictions reflected in this great book of Ruskin, and that is why it so captured me and made me transform my life. A poet is one who can call forth the good latent in the human breast.

The teachings of *Unto This Last* I understood to be:

1. That the good of the individual is contained in the good of all.
2. That a lawyer's work has the same value as the barber's in as much as all have the same right of earning their livelihood from their work.
3. That a life of labor, i.e. the life of the tiller of the soil and the handicraftsman, is the life worth living.

...I arose with the dawn, ready to reduce these principles to practice. [5]

Gandhi himself acknowledged the influence of Leo Tolstoy, particularly *The Kingdom of God is Within You.* It left an abiding impression on me before the independent thinking, profound morality, and the truthfulness of this book;

---

[5] *Mohandas K. Gandhi, An Autobiography: The Story of My Experiments with Truth,* trans. from the original in Gujarati by Mahadev Desai (Boston: Beacon Press, 1957), pp. 298-299. The first edition of Gandhi's Autobiography was published in two volumes in 1927 and 1929.

all the books given me by Mr. Coates seemed to pale into insignificance.[6] In his last letter, September 7, 1910, to Gandhi, Tolstoy expressing his appreciation of Gandhi's passive resistance movement as being important not only for India but for the whole humanity and stressing the relevance of 'satyagraha', states:

> ...What one calls non-resistance is in reality nothing else but the discipline of love... Christ knew... that the employment of violence is incompatible with love, which is the fundamental law of life... once violence is admitted... the law of love is thereby rendered futile.[7]

'Satyagraha' is popularly translated in English as passive resistance or non-cooperation. Such a translation hardly conveys its intrinsic meaning and value. In fact, there is nothing passive about it, nor is it a negative conception. It is a positive doctrine of work, organization, struggle, and resistance. It is passive insofar as armed resistance is concerned, but its moral resistance is positive, active, determined, and carries spiritual power as well. It is 'Truth Force'. "Satyagraha," Gandhi wrote, "is the vindication of truth not by infliction of suffering on the opponent but on one's self." The opponent must be 'weaned from error by patience and sympathy'. Weaned, not crushed ('Satya' means truth, the equivalent of love, and both are attributes of the soul; 'Agraha' is firmness or force.) Aptly echoing Gandhi's sentiments, Louis Fisher, the outstanding biographer of Gandhi, states that this weapon was employed both in South Africa and later in India not to humiliate or defeat the whites. Gandhi's innate desire was to convert them.

---

[6] lbid., pp. 137-138.

[7] *The Collected Works of Mahatma Gandhi,* Vol. X (New Delhi: Publications Division, Government of India, 1963), p. 512. My quotation is drawn from V.V. Ramana Murti's "Influence of Tolstoy on Gandhi's Political Technique and Thought" in *Gandhi and the West,* ed. C.D. Narasimhaiah (Mysore: University of Mysore), p. 165.

'Satyagraha' returns good for evil until the evildoer tires of evil.

Satyagraha received its first test when the *Transvaal Government Gazette* of August 22, 1906 published the draft of an act requiring all Indian men, women and children above the age of eight, to submit to official registration and fingerprinting on pain of fines. Despite the protest by Gandhi and his followers, the Asiatic Registration Act (also known as the 'Black Act') was passed on July 31, 1907. Gandhi was imprisoned – a beginning of many such imprisonments that would follow his life pattern in the service of humanity. In a contemporary article, Gandhi wrote that "The real road to happiness lies in going to jail and undergoing suffering and privations there in the interest of one's country and religion." Undoubtedly, the prisoner's soul was free. These views echo those of Henry David Thoreau's, the New England rebel, who wrote of his own prison experience. "I did not feel for a moment confined, and the walls seemed a great waste of stone and mortar." Now for the first time Gandhi read Thoreau's 'Civil Disobedience', the most electric of all Thoreau's essays, which reinforced ideas that Gandhi had already arrived at for himself – that it was more honorable to be right than to be law-abiding; that it was every man's right indeed, his duty to resist a tyrannical government, and that a minority of one could bring about a change in the government.

Gandhi called Thoreau's 'Civil Disobedience' a 'masterly treatise' which 'left a deep impression on him'. There was a Thoreau imprint on much that Gandhi did, as there was an Indian imprint on Thoreau; he and his friend Ralph Waldo Emerson had read the *Bhagavad* Gita among the Indian influences; Gandhi gives *Gita* a supreme position-and some of the sacred Hindu *Upanishads.* Thus Thoreau in Massachusetts borrowed from Gandhi's India and repaid the debt with words that reached Gandhi in a South African cell.[8]

Ironically, at the time he read Thoreau, Gandhi was in jail for denying unjust laws on moral grounds. Like Thoreau, Gandhi felt it more honorable to be right than to be law-

---

[8] Louis Fisher, *Gandhi,* p. 38

abiding. In 'Civil Disobedience', Thoreau asserts with a clear conscience that "The only obligation which I have a right to assume is to do at any time I think right."[9]

Though Gandhi never visited America, the two nineteenth-century American transcendentalists, Thoreau and Emerson, wielded powerful influence on the shaping of his thought and confirmation of his ideas. The several issues of *Indian Opinion,* which Gandhi founded in 1903 and edited for ten years in South Africa and which became the chief medium for pouring forth his soul, contain extracts from 'Civil Disobedience' and the founders' enthusiasm for Thoreau.

...Many years ago, there lived in America a great man named Henry David Thoreau. His writings are read and pondered over by millions of people. Some of them put his ideas into practice. Much importance is attached to his writings because Thoreau himself was a man who practiced what he preached. Impelled by a sense of duty, he wrote much against his own country, America. He considered a great sin that the Americans held many persons in the bond of slavery. He did not rest content with saying this, but took all other necessary steps to put a stop to this trade. One of those steps consisted in not paying any taxes to the State in which the slave trade was being carried on. He was imprisoned when he stopped paying the taxes due from him. The thoughts which occurred to him during this imprisonment were boldly original and were published in the form of a book. Historians say that the chief cause of the abolition of slavery in America was Thoreau's imprisonment and the publication by him of the book after his release. Both his example and writings are at present exactly applicable to the Indians in Transvaal. [10]

(Thoreau's 'Civil Disobedience', originally a lecture delivered in 1848 and first published in May 1849 in Elizabeth Peabody's symposium called *Aesthetic Papers,* articulates the

---

[9] *The Portable Thoreau,* ed. Carl Bode, rev. edn. (New York: The Viking Press, 1970), p. 111

[10] M.V.Karnath,*TheUnitedStatesandIndia,1776-1976* (Washington, D.C.: The Embassy of India, 1976), pp. 65-66

vehement protest of the Sage of Walden Pond against slavery and the invasion of Mexico.)

On October 5, 1907, in a letter that appeared in *Indian Opinion,* Gandhi re-emphasized the theme of 'Civil Disobedience': ...There is a deep-rooted superstition that a law cannot be disobeyed. It would be no small step forward for the community if this superstition were rooted out. When we shall have resisted the law to the last, we shall be regarded as so many Thoreaus in miniature. By this time, the readers of the *Opinion* must be aware of who Thoreau was.[11]

A week later, Gandhi was appealing to his countrymen in Transvaal to follow Thoreau's great example and refuse to accept some of the laws in South Africa whose sense was conveyed to the Indian community in a letter to Mr. Jan Smuts (who later became the country's prime minister).

...There is the great God to provide for us. A mere crumb of bread. He will give us at any other place as well. Once we are inspired by such a spirit, people will see how glorious our struggle can be. Such persons, like the brave Thoreau, will find jail to be a palace and the cry of challenge from Indians in prison shall pierce Mr. Smuts through and through.

As is well known, Gandhi was fighting against the apartheid laws of South Africa, against tremendous odds. His only weapon was 'Civil Disobedience'. For Gandhi, Thoreau was the teacher, the master, the man to be followed to the bitter end, one who confirmed Gandhi's own concept of 'Civil Disobedience'. The October 26, 1907 issue of *Indian Opinion* carried the following piece that further substantiates the significance of Thoreau:

...David Thoreau was a great writer, philosopher, poet, and withal the most practical man, that is, he taught nothing he was not prepared to practice himself. He was one of the greatest and most moral men America has produced. At the time of the abolition of slavery movement, he wrote his famous essay 'On the Duty of Civil Disobedience'. He went to Gaol for the sake of his principles and suffering humanity. His essay has therefore been sanctified by suffering.

---

[11] Ibid., p. 66.

Moreover, it is written for all time. Its incisive logic is unanswerable.[12]

Roger Baldwin, Chairman of American Civil Liberties Union, as Gandhi's co-passenger on a train ride through France in 1931, noticed the twentieth-century leader carrying Thoreau's essay. To Baldwin's remark that Thoreau was an extremist, Gandhi gently asserted that the New England Brahmin's essay epitomized 'the essence of his political philosophy not only as India's struggle related to the British but as to his own views of the relation of citizens to Government'.[13] Later, Gandhi in his 1942 appeal 'To American Friends' affirmed that the essay furnished him a scientific confirmation of what he' was doing in South Africa, needless further to reiterate that 'Thoreau came into Gandhi's life at a very crucial time in the development of the Satyagraha civil resistance'.15 And "Gandhi must have marked that the conditions in South Africa were not dissimilar to the conditions obtaining in mid-century America against which the New England revolutionary was declaiming."[14]

---

[12] lbid., pp. 66-67

[13] *Thoreau Society Bulletin,* XI, 2 (April 1945) as quoted in George Hendrick's essay, 'The Influence of Thoreau's "Civil Disobedience" on Gandhi's Satyagraha', *New England Quarterly,* XXIX (1959), p. 462.

[14] Seshachari, *Gandhi, and the American Scene: An Intellectual History and Inquiry* (Bombay: Nachiketa Publications Ltd., 1969), pp. 20-21.

A Passage Now from America via South Africa to India!

Mahatma Gandhi dominated the twentieth-century scene with his marvelous symbolic acts like the Great Salt March of 1930, his untiring role in making India achieve freedom from Great Britain, his message to the world incorporating principles of courage, nonviolence, and truth, with his saintly life guided by a search for truth, believing truth could be known only through tolerance and concern for his fellow men, with his conquering fear in himself and teaching others to master fear.

A passage to America! A wispy brown man in a loincloth began to capture the American imagination and consciousness between 1919 and 1969. He was portrayed in many contexts: in regard to the fate and future of British and Western colonialism, with respect to religious issues, in regard to war and to the economic future of the world. He came into American consciousness particularly with respect to the challenge to British imperialism. In the American mind, Gandhi personified the anti-colonial struggle and independence movement. Being far removed from American experience, his struggles seemed more interesting than instructive and functional. On the official level, Gandhi was respected as 'the authentic voice of India', and most of the consular reports tended to be pro-British. Yet American senators gave moral support to Indian independence. Gandhi commanded respect and admiration. "His many-sidedness still baffled the average American, but the very enigma of Gandhi became the controlling part of the American's image of the Indian leader."[15] He was portrayed as "Patriot martyr, high-souled idealist, and archtraitor, evangelist, pacific quietist, and truculent tub-thumper and revolutionist, subverter of empires and founder of creeds, a man of tortuous wiles and stratagems, or, to use his own phrase, 'a single-minded seeker after truth'."[16] In 1920s, however, pacific crusaders like Charles Clayton Morrison, editor of the *Christian Century,* Rev. John Haynes Holmes of *Unity,* who later published a book, *My Gandhi,* began to venerate Gandhi. "We may not comprehend him; we cannot ignore him." Thus the *Christian Century* editorialized in 1924. "Frequently we are troubled by the suspicion that we have as a contemporary one of the outstanding figures in the spiritual history of our race, but that, because of veils of distance, of culture, and of false witness, we are prevented from knowledge of a life of immense importance."

The outstanding contribution of Gandhian philosophy and techniques to the American political and social thought – nearly two hundred years after the American Revolution – resulted when Martin Luther King Jr. looked up to Gandhi for the strategy to liberate fellow blacks from their plight of discrimination. When King arrived in New Delhi on an extended visit, his first words were a tribute to Mahatma Gandhi.

"To other countries," King said, "I may go as a tourist, but to India I come as a pilgrim. This is because India means to me Mahatma Gandhi, a truly great man of the age." The Indian trip was a unique spiritual catharsis to King.

It was then, in 1959, that he met many old disciples of Gandhi and studied at first hand the Gandhian technique of non-violent non-cooperation. He left India convinced 'that non-violent resistance is the most potent weapon available to oppressed people in their struggle for freedom. It was a

---

[15] Ibid., p. 21
[16] Ibid., p. 51

marvelous thing to see the results of a non-violent campaign'.[17]

King first encountered Gandhi's image when he was a student at Crozen Theological Seminary. A fleeting introduction it was. Yet he was stimulated by the powerful lecturing of Dr. Mordecai W. Johnson, President of Howard University, who had attended a conference at Gandhi's ashram (retreat) in Sevagram and had stayed in India to become convinced that the movement there offered a model for his own people. Even prior to that, King had learnt of Gandhi's philosophy of non-violence in a course offered by Prof. George W. Davis, but then it had not struck fire. It was in Dr. Johnson's presentation that 'Gandhi's spiritual leadership and pacifist techniques attained an immediate and luminescent dimension'. King later admitted that Johnson's lecture on Gandhi's message was so profound and electrifying that he left the meeting and brought half a dozen books on Gandhi's life and works. [18] In fact, as early as 1932, Reinhold Niebuhr, the foremost American theologian of the century, offered suggestions about the aptness of the Gandhian methods to the struggle for racial equality in the U.S.A. "That Gandhian way would be the very means needed to extricate blacks from their lowly position in the American caste system."[19] Echoing Gandhi's sentiments, King later declared that 'our goal is not to defeat or humiliate the white man, but to win his friendship and love'.

Martin Luther King, the man who employed the philosophy and the technique of 'Gandhi's nonviolent

---

[17] Edmund Candler, 'Mahatma Gandhi', *Atlantic Monthly,* 130 (July 1922),105, as quoted in *The Americanization of Gandhi: Images of the Mahatma,* ed. with an introductory essay by Charles Chatfield (New York: Garland Publishing, Inc., 1976), pp. 29-30.

[18] M.V. Karnath, *The United States and India,* p. 69

[19] David L. Lewis, *King, a Critical Biography* (Praeger, 1970), p. 3. Quoted in Om Dikshit's 'The Impact of Mahatma Gandhi on Martin Luther King, Jr.', *Negro History Bulletin,* Vol. No. 38, No. 2, 1975, p. 342

resistance to the social and racial conflict in America and who, like Gandhi, became a living symbol of the fight for the human in man, was assassinated like Gandhi, in the midst of the very tensions to which he had tried to bring a word of justice and peace'.[20]

Thus, in Thoreau, Gandhi, and King, we come a full circle.

The thinking behind 'Civil Disobedience' and nonviolent protest goes back a long time, with Indians and Americans contributing much to its development. Who is to say how long India and America have shared ideas? Gandhi's political philosophy lodged in two central constructs, 'Ahimsa' (nonviolence) and 'Satyagrha' (truth, love, or soul force) "embody the highest values of most religions and most advanced civilizations. Their appeal transcends cultural and national differences and has a contemporary significance as arms races and superpower nuclear inventories escalate."

"...Perhaps we need to adapt Gandhi's method from a curative to a preventive function. Instead of attempting to deter nuclear attack after it has been launched, the modem strategy of nonviolence could focus more fully and effectively on reduction and elimination of the instruments of conflict."[21]

The real meaningfulness and relevance of Gandhi's teachings for each of us – his emphasis on kindness, honesty, humility, nonviolence, and the exaltation of the individual human spirit-obliterates geographical boundaries and carries with it a universal appeal. 'The organic connection between religion, or at least ethics, and politics constitutes a lingering hope for survival in the nuclear age. For Gandhi to have made

---

[20] David L. Lewis, *King, a Critical Biography* (Praeger, 1970), p. 3. Quoted in Om Dikshit's 'The Impact of Mahatma Gandhi on Martin Luther King, Jr.', *Negro History Bulletin,* Vol. No. 38, No. 2, 1975, p. 342

[21] Reinhold Niebuhr, *Moral Man and Immoral Society* (New York: Charles Scribner's and Sons, 1960), pp., 251-254. Quoted in Om Dikshit's 'The Impact of Mahatma Gandhi on Martin Luther King, Jr.', p. 342

this connection must be considered an abiding virtue of his work in today's disordered world.' "The hypothesis of 'peace-through-force' has been experimentally disproved throughout the whole of history, that 'nightmare from which we cannot awaken'. Connecting peace with *ahimsa* and *satya* is an alternative hypothesis which has been tried only a few times with mixed, but not disastrous results. Perhaps it is time to give this concept of peace another chance..."[22]

We may still assure the writer to the Public Forum of *The Salt Lake Tribune* hope and let him realize that there are many in the world who are aware of his concerns because they are their concerns too. Sir Richard Attenborough has succeeded in creating a surge of interest in the personality, philosophy, historical role, and vision of Mahatma Gandhi.

The two largest democracies in the world have demonstrated through their histories and concerns how political and social problems can be solved peacefully. East is East; West is West. They do share ideas for mutual aspirations. Gandhi linked the thought of East and West in his search for universal truth.

I wish to express my sincere gratitude to the Faculty Committee for recognizing the value of my lecture topic and letting me take all of you as my co-passengers in circumnavigating the worlds of Thoreau, Gandhi, and King.

---

[22] Maurice Friedman in *Nonviolence After Gandhi-A Study of Martin Luther King, Jr.,* ed. by G. Ramachandran and T.K. Mahadevan (New Delhi: Gandhi Peace Foundation, 1968), p. 12

East and West: A Time to Meet

The West is passing through a new Renaissance due to the sudden entry into its consciousness of a whole new world of ideas, shapes, and fancies. Even as its consciousness was enlarged in the period of the Renaissance by the revelation of the classical culture of Greece and Rome, there is a sudden growth of the spirit affected by the new inheritance of Asia with which India is linked up. For the first time in the history of mankind, the consciousness of the unity of the world has dawned on us. Whether we like it or not, East and West have come together and can no more part.

> – S. Radhakrishnan

Today, in the Centennial year of Southern Utah University's founding founded by Mormon pioneers – we have on our campus students from the East – Koreans, Chinese, and Japanese. Today, in the 250th anniversary of its founding, Princeton University, founded by Presbyterians to school white Protestant males in morality and academics, has become a more secular institution that offers its diverse student body a smorgasbord of religious communities to choose from... where Hindus and Jews share a meal at the Center for Jewish life, where Mormons, Quakers, Bahais, and Zen Buddhists, though few in number, congregate for prayer, worship, and meditation. Today, addressing you and sharing his East-West experiences, observations, and academic training is a Hindu Brahmin who considers himself a modern-day pioneer of southern Utah, having taught here for more than two decades courses in American literature, British literature, and Eastern literatures in translation – Indian, Chinese, and Japanese literatures – with profound satisfaction and dignity. Today, you are being addressed by a speaker who has origins in the ancient land of India, the country that Christopher Columbus wanted to discover, the country that the great American bard Walt Whitman in the late 19th century invokes symbolically as the abode of 'spirit'; his poem 'Passage to India' provided a symbol of the meeting of the East and the West, 'heralding the cultural and spiritual union of mankind'.

Is the East 'spiritual', the West 'materialistic?' Is the East passive, the West aggressive? Is all mysticism in the East, all rationalism in the West? The human order is so 'East' here means essentially India, China, and Japan; 'West' means chiefly Western Europe and North America. Though I may be making references to Chinese thought and philosophies such as Taoism, Confucianism, and Buddhism, and to Japanese literary influences as well as to Zen Buddhism, I wish, however, to focus more on Indian thought and Hindu scriptures; moreover, 'in Asia, India has played the part of Greece in Europe and we know to what extent we are still indebted to Greece, however unconsciously'. (Ananda K. Coomaraswamy in Christy's "The Asia Legacy and American Life", p. 219) There has long been a tendency to think in terms of a dichotomy between East and West, presupposing two mutually opposed cultural sets of values labeled 'occidental' and 'oriental'. This 'sort of explanation by paired opposites is now regarded as too simple: the cultures of the 'orient' and 'occident' are too diversified and each one is extremely complex'. (Nakamura, p. 1)

The broad startling distinctions between the 'East' and the 'West', though troubling and disconcerting to the discerning and enlightened observers and students of societies, do remain. The psychic traits may be generally identified to the following effect. An Oriental is contemplative, placid, gentle, courteous, patient, introspective, conservative, philosophical, passive, negative, feminine, submissive, mythological, and pessimistic. An Occidental, on the other hand, is active, restless, sincere, impatient, progressive, individualistic, ethical, autonomous, strong, aggressive, positive, masculine,

33

masterful, liberal, scientific, and optimistic. These classifications, however, do not differentiate between the intelligentsia and the mass of the people. Yet they present to us an overall picture, however unsatisfactory it may be. P. C. Mozoomdar succinctly states the distinction: "In the West, you observe, watch, and act. In the East, we contemplate and commune, and suffer ourselves to be carried away by the spirit of the universe. In the West, you wrest from nature her secrets. You conquer her. She makes you wealthy and prosperous; you look upon her as your slave, and sometimes fail to realize her sacredness. In the East, nature is our eternal sanctuary, the soul is our everlasting temple, and the sacredness of God's creation is only next to the sacredness of God himself. In the West, you love equality. You respect man. You seek justice. In the East, love is the fulfilment of the law; we have hero worship. We behold God in humanity. In the West, you establish the moral law; you insist upon propriety of conduct. You are governed by public opinion. In the East we aspire, perhaps vainly aspire, after absolute self-conquest, and the holiness which makes God its model. In the West, you work incessantly and your work is worship. In the East, we meditate and worship for long hours, and worship is our work." (Quoted in Sidney Lewis Gulick's "The East and the West", p. 119)

I would also wish to present yet another view of a respected Indian historian K. M. Panikkar – a view that is essentially realistic. "The claim that India is spiritual and that Europe is materialistic is no more than a degraded and meaningless affectation of religiosity, a mere adherence to forms the meaning of which is utterly lost to the many. Any serious study of European life would convince the enquirer that side by side with the grossest I would also wish to present yet another view of a respected Indian historian K. M. Panikkar – a view that is essentially realistic. "The claim that India is spiritual and that Europe is materialistic is no more than a degraded and meaningless affectation of religiosity, a mere adherence to forms the meaning of which is utterly lost to the many. Any serious study of European life would convince the enquirer that side by side with the grossest materialism, with the brazen worship of mammon – which is by no means less prevalent in India – there exists in Europe a spirit of disciplined service, a desire for the well-being of mankind as such, a deep sensitiveness to suffering and misery born of profound humanism which constitute a unique translation of the religion of the spirit in practical life." (Gulick, "The East and the West", p. 120) Perhaps this is the picture of the post-colonial independent India with more than 960 million people with middle class in several strata representing one-third the population – almost the entire population of the U.S. – that is greatly drawn to materialism; the affluent minority cling to their riches tenaciously while the wretchedly poor continue to be passive, impoverished, and resign themselves to their unalterable 'karma'.

We may recognize, if we wish, unbridgeable differences in the dichotomy – the East and the West. We may, if we desire, like to consider 'the East and the West' as 'two vast psychological continents... groups of psychological peaks concealed by mists of misunderstanding or clouds of ignorance'. What a fascinating challenge to all of us to probe, recognize, and realize the foundation of a common human nature!

It is legitimate to consider 'East' and 'West' as relative terms or constructs – despite differences – and to treat them as complementary. We now live in an age of global economy, satellite-beamed instant cover age of world events, and continual educational and cultural exchanges. At this stage in history, no civilization needs to be isolated and self-satisfied with its own accomplishments. "Our age is dominated by this will for universalism." To ignore the East – the oriental world – its rich cultural and literary traditions and its philosophical contributions would be 'to neglect many of the finest possessions of mankind'. The orient charms the occident greatly because it is so different – 'mysterious, elusive, and puzzling'. No wonder over several centuries, engaging conversation has been going on between the various cultures of East and West – 'to a limited degree ever since Jesuits at the courts of the Indian Moguls and the Ming Emperors of China first made available to Western readers the classical writings of these two great Oriental civilizations. Thomas Berry clearly and convincingly explains that:

> The human order is so rich in its racial, linguistic, cultural, and political expression that no one people or culture or state can carry the full splendor of man, just as no flower can carry the full splendor of the world of flowers. The fullness of wisdom cannot be carried exclusively by any one person or age or expressed in one language. Different literary and artistic talents are distributed throughout the world so that only the Chinese of the T'ang and Sung periods in China could produce the poetry and painting characteristic of those periods. Only the Japanese could produce the 'no drama' of the medieval period... None but the Indian people could produce the Upanishadic speculations or the Vedanta philosophy. Only the Buddhist world could produce the philosophy of Vasubandhu. (Wm. Theodore de Bary, Approaches to Oriental Classics, p. 17)

The complex ideas of the Vedanta philosophy of the Hindus are remarkably and eloquently articulated in a dialog form, compressed language, between Lord Krishna and Arjuna, the warrior in *The Bhagavad Gita*, which has been translated from Sanskrit into English and other Western languages since the English version was published by Charles Wilkins in 1785. The 20th-century British novelist Aldous Huxley described *The Gita* as 'one of the most sublime creations in the world'. The positive response of *The Gita* reflects Western appreciation of the broader Indian culture. Westerners have been discovering the exotic and splendid India since antiquity-members of Alexander the Great's expedition, in the fourth century B.C., recorded their impressions in terms of fabulous exoticism.

In 19th century America, Thoreau, Emerson, and Walt Whitman demonstrate unequivocally the influence of Indian thought and their awareness of many works of Asian literature, as a consequence of circulation of translation of The Bhagavad Gita by Sir William Jones, a judge of the Supreme Court in Calcutta and an erudite linguist of the time, and Charles Wilkins, a merchant in the service of the East India Company in Bengal in late 1700s. These translations formed the basis of modern Western conceptions of ancient Indian culture.

German writers Schlegel, Humboldt, and Goethe as well as American writers Thoreau, Emerson, and Whitman paid close attention to the Indian literature. "Among the several works of Asian literature that were studied in Concord, Massachusetts, in the mid-nineteenth century, none was more influential than the Bhagavad Gita (The Song of God); this is more a philosophical dialog rather than a religious treatise or scripture. In his journal of 1845, Emerson wrote: I owed – my friend and I owed – a magnificent day to the Bhagavat Gita. It was the first of books; it was as if an empire spoke to us, nothing small or unworthy, but large, serene, consistent, the voice of the old intelligence which another age and climate had pondered and thus disposed of the same questions which exercise us. Emerson's chief interest is in Lord Krishna's teaching that works must be done without thought of reward and that a person may have a tranquil mind even in activity. Krishna's teaching cuts across religious, geographical, and cultural boundaries – transcendental.

"In Walden, the book named for the pond in Concord where Thoreau lived from 1845 to 1847, he expresses his profound response to that as he observes ice being cut from Walden Pond to be transported to India by New England merchants:

Thus it appears that the sweltering inhabitants of Charleston and New Orleans, of Madras and Bombay and Calcutta, drank at my well. In the morning, I bathe my intellect in the stupendous and cosmogonal philosophy of the Bhagavat Gita, since whose composition years of the gods have elapsed, and in comparison with which our modern world and its literature seem puny and trivial; the pure Walden water is mingled with the sacred water of the Ganges. (Barbara Stoler Miller's translation of The Bhagavad-Gita, p.156)

Let me parenthetically add that the Ganges, specifically at Benares, the holy city of the Hindus, according to several recent scientific studies, is dangerously polluted. Pollution is physical and chemical; the river still retains the purity of its sacredness. Barbara Stoler Miller further enthusiastically adds that: "Walden was for Thoreau a spiritual retreat where he strove to deepen his understanding to gain release from the terrible bondage of life's compelling illusions. In Indian terms, it was the retreat of a yogi who carefully practiced spiritual discipline." (p. 161)

Thoreau and other transcendentalists felt that the Divine was open to them at all time, and His form reflects the individual's perception. Perhaps this is why Thoreau was drawn to Eastern religions and their philosophies. Instead of describing man as a sinner in need of repentance, Hinduism specifically celebrates all that man can be, and that through self-discipline, one can transcend one's human limitations and contact the gods.

"The Hindus are more serenely and thoughtfully religious than the Hebrews. Repentance is not a free and fair highway to God. A wise man will dispense with repentance ...God prefers that you approach him thoughtful, not penitent... It is only by forgetting yourself that you draw near to Him."

Thoreau had freed himself from the idea of 'an arbitrary deity', and this sense of openness and positivity demonstrated that his religious beliefs were leaning towards the East. The basic Indian concept of God can be stated as follows: "The world is God and God is the soul," and that idea, along with the notion of self-transcendence, appealed to Thoreau, who felt that instead of concentrating on man as a sinner, one must concentrate on man as a special divinity." And to a large extent, Thoreau focused on two areas of thought: Hinduism and Confucian writings.

The French writer Romain Rolland, who has been deeply influenced by Indian thought, affirms: "There are a certain number of us in Europe for whom the civilization of Europe is no longer enough."

The Irish Literary Renaissance, with its central figures of W. B. Yeats and George W. Russell (AE), is molded by Eastern conceptions. There are many literary men today in Europe and America who are greatly and spiritually influenced by Indian thought and classics and look to them for inspiration in our present troubles. Aldous Huxley in his books, Eyeless in Gaza and Ends and Means, invites our attention to the discipline essential for spiritual insight and persuades us for the acceptance of the Yoga method. The influence of Indian thought is not so much a model to be copied as a dye which permeates. Sir Charles Eliot, in his work Hinduism and Buddhism, confesses that: "I cannot share the confidence in the superiority of Europeans and their ways which is prevalent in the West. European civilization is not satisfying and Asia can still offer something more attractive to many who are far from Asiatic in spirit." (Quoted in Radhakrishnan's Eastern Religion and Western Thought, pp. 250-51)

During the past half century, scholars have investigated, recognized, and acknowledged T. S. Eliot's deep interest in Indian philosophical systems and their influence on his poetry and drama. The East-West interpenetration leads to the discovery of an East-West ideosynthesis in this Nobel laureate's work.

Eliot declared in no uncertain terms:

> In the literature of Asia is great poetry. There is also profound wisdom and some very difficult metaphysics. Long ago, I studied the ancient Indian languages, and while I was chiefly interested at that time in philosophy, I read a little poetry too; and I know that my own poetry shows the influence of Indian thought and sensibility. (Notes Toward the Definition of Culture, p. 113)

P. S. Sri in his scholarly investigation of Eliot's work that is imbued with direct references to the Hindu and Buddhist

39

texts from The Waste Land and Four Quartets through The Cocktail Party demonstrates 'Eliot's implicit fusion of Indian philosophical themes and symbols with the Western worldview in an organic whole... the universal insights of Vedanta and Buddhism, impermanence and suffering, along with the symbolism of the wheel, maya, and the still point, in terms of Eliot's acute awareness of the transience of life and the tyranny of time... in Sanskrit terminology, Eliot could well be described as risi and kavi poet, sage, prophet, and visionary'. (T. S. Eliot, Vedanta and Buddhism, dust jacket account) Sri further clarifies that Eliot's poetry is invested with beauty and a penetrating power because 'he has perceived the perennial and most ancient truth of humanity and invoked THAT which is universal and eternal, common to both the East and the West'. (p. 124) Eliot admitted: "I am not a Buddhist, but some of the early Buddhist scriptures affect me as parts of the Old Testament." (The Use of Poetry and the Use of Criticism, p. 91) Eliot believed that the Buddha's Fire Sermon 'corresponds in importance to the Sermon on the Mount'. ('Notes of The Waste Land' in The Complete Poems and Plays, p. 79)

Another American Nobel laureate who read numerous volumes on Oriental religions and cultures is Eugene O'Neill. Perhaps this 20th-century playwright was more of an Orientalist than Emerson or Thoreau; as briefly mentioned before, Emerson was interested in a number of Hindu concepts – 'the Vedantic theory of the Absolute Unity in Brahman, the idea of self-reliance and Karma, the transmigration and immortality of the soul, the personality and impersonality of God, the doctrine of emanation – all of which were to find later expression in 'Over-Soul', 'Self-Reliance', 'God', 'Plato', and other essays. It was the idea of Maya or illusion, the pivotal principle of the Vedantic school of Hindu philosophy, which most thoroughly, captured his imagination'. (Pachori, p.45) Thoreau, on the other hand, focused on Confucian writings as well. (Confucius, 551-479 B.C.E., China's greatest philosopher, revered throughout China, never claiming to be a God, centered his teachings around humanity, filial piety, loyalty, decorum and natural integrity, and dignity of all men; self-cultivation, regulation of the family, social civility, moral education, well-being of the people, governance of the state, the universal peace. His humanism has been admired by generations of scholars and thinkers, East and West. Confucius wrote that 'by nature all men are pretty much alike; it is by custom and habit that they are set apart'.) On the other hand, O'Neill was attracted more to the philosophical Taoism rather than to the Confucian humanism. (In recent years, Taoism has received unexpected attention from Western intellectuals because of its formative influence on the Japanese school of Zen Buddhism. Wing-Tsit Chan in his Preface to his translation The Way of Lao Tzu – Taote Ching asserts that 'no one can understand China or be an intelligent citizen of the world without some knowledge of Lao Tzu, also called the Taote Ching – The Classic of the Way and Its Virtue...'

"Chinese civilization and the Chinese character would have been utterly different if the book Lao Tzu had never been written... No one can hope to understand Chinese philosophy, religion, government, art, medicine, and even cooking without a real appreciation of the profound philosophy taught in this little book." p. 3)

While Confucianism emphasizes social order and an active life, Taoism, on the other hand, concentrates on individual life and tranquility. O'Neill admits that 'the mysticism of Lao-tse and Chuang-Tzu probably interested me more than any other Oriental writing'; O'Neill's fascination with the Orient lay in its mystical speculations about man, God and reality – "The illusory phenomenal world, the unreal ego, the ensnarements of desire, the wandering soul, and the impersonal forces behind life." (Robinson, Eugene O'Neill and Oriental Thought, p. 22) Robinson concludes his stupendous study on O'Neill's oriental thought by stating that the playwright's appeal 'will no doubt increase for Orientals, especially those westernized enough to experience a similar conflict between their traditional values and the goals offered by another civilization. Universal as O'Neill's work may be, it is of course unlikely to bridge the gap between East and West; but his divided vision may further mutual understanding by offering deep and subtle statements of the problem'. (p. 186) The hero of O'Neill's first full-length play to be produced-Andrew Mayo in Beyond the Horizon – emphatically proclaimed his idealization of 'the beauty of the far off and unknown, the mystery and spell of the East which lures me in the books I've read'.

American Modernist writers discovered the Far East at the tum of the Twentieth Century. Ezra Pound's receipt of Ernest Fenollosa's notes on Chinese poetry and Japanese Noh drama in the autumn of 1913 signals the American writers' readiness to examine the Far East is in some ways a continuation of Commodore Perry's opening of Japan in 1853. Pound's publication in Pre-Fenollosa haiku in Poetry in April 1913 is perhaps another landmark:

In a Station of the Metro
The apparition of these faces in the crowd;
Petals on a wet black bough

Through travel, literature, philosophy, education, religion, and fine and decorative arts, Americans involved themselves in the East, particularly China and Japan. Ba yard Taylor, who accompanied Perry, published his impressions of the voyage; he lectured in nearly hundred American cities and towns. When the first Japanese delegation came to New York, Walt Whitman watched their Broadway Parade, and his poem about it appeared in *The New York Times* of June 27, 1860. In 1876, the Centennial Exposition in Philadelphia featured Japanese Pavilion. In 1877, President Grant met with the Prince Regent of China and the Emperor of Japan, and his trip electrified Americans. Henry Adams traveled to Japan to observe customs, nature, and art in 1880s. Chinese and Japanese themes inundated fiction and the theater, with The Mikado. This past summer the Utah Shakespearean Festival successfully presented the contemporary version of this musical – and "Madam Butterfly" rising to immense popularity. Harvard-trained Ernest Fenollosa became a professor of philosophy at the Imperial University in Tokyo. His legacy of Chinese poetry and Japanese Noh drama received Ezra Pound's best attention. The other American modernists, H.D., Wallace Stevens, William Carlos Williams, Amy Lowell, E.E. Cummings and Marianne Moore made serious and largely unobserved use of Japanese and Chinese art and literature, partly based on their own encounters with Eastern art, literature, and philosophy.

In the final analysis, the meeting of East and West is not a matter of ideas at all, although what I have traced and portrayed so far presents a nebulous picture of miniature portraits of intellectuals, writers, and travelers' attempts and ventures. When the encounters occur at the level of ideas, the result tends to be either polemic, proselytizing, or premature, synthesizing, and superficial equating. As Harvard-educated theologian, Harvey Cox in his informative and exploratory study based on several profound experiences and exposures to 'New Orientalism' affirms, "We have now come to a time when the meeting must take place not in the realm of ideas but in the lives of actual persons living in real societies – that is, in the flesh. When that begins to happen, as I believe it can, then eventually the ideas will follow."

"He that doeth the will of God shall know the doctrine." (Turning East, p. 145)

But now there are a thousand channels through which the influences flow from one to another. Oriental or eastern ideas, outlooks, and attitudes throughout the West, particularly in the U.S., are diffused through mass media; extensive CNN worldwide coverage not only of news but, more importantly, of in-depth presentation of cultural and social events, frequent exchange of cultural delegations, presentation of folk and classical dance performances and music concerts by visiting artistes, sponsored by several immigrant cultural and social organizations in several major U.S. cities; yearlong festivals like the 'Festival of India' in 1985 and 1986, the largest concentration of Indian art and culture ever assembled in the

United States included special exhibitions of painting, sculpture and the performing arts in New York, Washington, and forty other cities from coast to coast, which put India into the consciousness of a good many American who have not paid much attention to the place before, educating them, as Alistair Cook did every Sunday night in his introductions to 'The Jewel in the Crown', movies like Richard Attenborough's Oscar-award-winning 'Gandhi', David Lean's 'A Passage to India', Bernardo Bertolucci's Academy-award-winner 'The Last Emperor'.

Moreover, America's changing religious landscape further testifies to my thesis that East-West have met – or, I may rephrase to emphasize that it is time. The important catalyst in bringing the world's religious traditions to North America was the passage of the 1965 immigration act-proposed by President John F. Kennedy and signed into law by Lyndon B. Johnson. The recent burst of Asian immigration and the rise of a new Asian American population-from about one million in 1965 to 7.3 million in 1990 further brought the East closer on social and cultural planes. New immigration, not only from Asia, but from the Middle East, Latin America, the Caribbean, and Eastern Europe, has begun to change the cultural and religious landscape of the U.S. in dramatic ways. Major U.S. cities such as New York, Boston, Los Angeles, Chicago, San Francisco, Houston, and Salt Lake City, can justifiably now take pride in being hospitable to Indian, Chinese, Japanese, Thai, Korean, Vietnamese restaurants and cultural organizations. These organizations sponsor professional dancers, musicians from their native countries and also promote local talent. We have now 'Little Indias' and 'Chinatowns'. Diana L. Eck, Professor of Comparative Religions and Indian Studies at Harvard University, in her article, 'Religious America: Perspectives on Pluralism', clarifies that for most of us, "New England calls to mind the white steeples and town greens of its colonial heritage. But today the ornate white temple-tower of a new Hindu temple, decorated with the many images of Hindu deities, rises amidst the maples of Ashland, a Boston suburb, not far from the starting point of the Boston marathon… On the final day of the consecration rites more than 3,000 Boston area Hindus, all in a festive spirit, circled the temple in a colorful procession, following twelve Hindu priests, each bearing on his head a large pot of consecrated water. The waters used for this ceremony were brought to Ashland from the Ganges River in India – and from the Mississippi, the Missouri, the Merrimac, and the Colorado rivers in the U.S." (p. 1) Yes, the East and the West have joined. "The mingling of the Ganges and the Mississippi powerfully evoked the sources of life and tradition that will nurture this Hindu community as it takes root in America." "…North of Boston, in the old industrial city of Lynn, a young Cambodian man who had come to the U.S. as a refugee is ordained as a Buddhist monk. His head shaven, he kneels to receive his robes amidst a Cambodian community that now has three temples in the northern outskirts of Boston. On a steamy summer day, more than a hundred Chinese Buddhists from the temple communities in Quincy and Lexington charter a boat to the outer waters of Boston harbor to release live fish and lobsters back into the sea, a traditional act that expresses compassion for all living things. This is New England in the 1990s. The whole world of religious diversity is here." (p. 2-3)

These specific instances of commingling graciously illustrate the coming together of the East and the West. At least it is so in America. As Professor Eck's account suggests, Cambridge, Massachusetts, 'provides an extraordinarily fertile field for pursuing an inquiry into neo-Oriental religious movements – International Society for Krishna Consciousness; Zen Center, furnished with black silk cushions, bells, and appropriately wizened and wise-looking resident master, and a visiting Zen swordplay instructor; International Student Meditation Center, founded several years ago by the Maharishi Mahesh Yogi, the best known of the swamis of the late '60s, where one can go to be initiated into the mysteries of TM; the Dharma House, founded recently by Chogyam Trungpa Rinpoche, the Tibetan

Buddhist lama, Tai Chi exhibits, sitar concerts." (Cox, Turning East, pp. 10-11)

Harvey Cox recognizes that in recent years, 'Cambridge has also become something its Calvinistic founders could hardly have foreseen. It is one of the four or five most thriving American centers of the neo-oriental religious surge. This should not be surprising since Cambridge is full of just the kind of people to whom these movements appeal mainly young, usually white, and almost always of middle-class background'. (p. 10) Cox further quips that his acquaintance, who recently returned from Benares, the Holy City of India, where millions come to bathe in the sacred waters of the Ganges, after taking a look around Cambridge, promptly rechristened it 'Benares-on-the-Charles'.

Several 20th-century global events also must have contributed to and accelerated the coming together of the East and the West. The First World War, the Second World War, Mahatma Gandhi's use of the force of 'nonviolence' (ahimsa) and 'satyagraha' (soul force) in gaining India's independence from the British and the concomitant disintegration of colonialism, the Korean War, the Vietnam War, the lifting of China's bamboo curtain, the melting of Iron Curtain, the Tiananmen Square democracy movement demonstrations in Beijing, China – all these have a significant role. India's Mahatma Gandhi, Satyajit Ray, Zubin Mehta, Ravi Shankar caught the cultural consciousness; on the spiritual plane, Transcendental Meditation, Yoga, Zen Buddhism have caught the imagination of the Americans. They are no more exotic. They are here. I am delighted to let my audience know that we have in Cedar City a Yoga and Meditation Center – Blue Heron Center – thanks to Terri Lauterbach Cotts.

Dr. Deepak Chopra, the Indian spiritual healer, who quite dexterously combines western medicine with Indian metaphysics with his in-depth study of India's traditional 'ayurveda', tells the Americans of 'spirit/body connection', though regarded skeptically by the scientific community and medical practitioners. After all, science may never be able to pin down the benefits of spirituality. The June 24, 1996 issue of *Time* magazine has its cover page announce: "Faith and Healing: Can Spirituality Promote Health?" A growing and surprising body of scientific evidence says that prayer, faith, and spirituality really improves one's physical health. Sister Judian Breitenbach, a Poor Handmaids of Jesus Christ nun who heads the Healing Arts Center in Mishawaka, Illinois, says: "We're moving toward the integration of the East and West, and it's happening through health care." (p. 65)

Dr. David Larson, a research psychiatrist formerly at the National Institutes of Health, confesses that 'we physicians are culturally insensitive about the role of religion... It is very important to many of our patients and not important to lots of doctors'. Jon Kabat-Zuin has applied Zen concepts to stress reduction at the University of Massachusetts Medical Center. It is generally reported that one senses a closeness to God while meditating. It is generally believed that patients can successfully battle a number of stress-related ills by practicing a simple form of meditation.

Marty Kaplan, who started out a nice Jewish boy from Newark, New Jersey, secularized by Harvard, a former speechwriter for Vice President Walter Mondale and Hollywood Studio executive, a screenwriter and producer, in his testimony admits.

"What attracted me to meditation was its apparent religious neutrality. You don't have to believe in anything; all you have to do is do it. Unwittingly, I was engaging in a practice that has been at the heart of religious mysticism for millenniums. To separate twenty minutes from the day with silence and intention is to worship, whether you call that or not. To be awakened to the miracle of existence – to experience, being not only in roses and sunsets but right now as something not out there but in here – this is the road less traveled, the path of pilgrim, the quest. The God I have found is common to Moses and Muhammad, to Buddha and Jesus. It is known to every mystic tradition... used to think of psychic phenomena as New Age flimflam. I used to think of reincarnation as a myth. I used to think the soul was a metaphor. Now I know there is a God – my God, in here, demanding not faith but experience, an inexhaustible wonder at the richness of this very moment. Now I know there is a consciousness that transcends science, a consciousness toward which our species is sputteringly evolving, a welcome development spurred ironically by our generational rendezvous with mortality." (Kaplan, Time, June 24, 1996, p. 62)

Information and study are paths leading to understanding and, fortunately, we in the West are now willing to study the East more thoroughly than we have been in the past. Sue Browder in her informative article 'Relieving Chronic Pain without Drugs' in the November 1996 issue of *Reader's Digest* clarifies that many leading chronic-pain clinics are promoting and encouraging patients to cope with pain using drug-free therapies. "Treatments once considered offbeat, such as bio feedback and meditation, are being used at major medical centers across the country, offering new hope to the ten to thirty percent of Americans who suffer pain so debilitating it disrupts their lives." 'Mindfulness Meditation' and Chinese 'Acupuncture' are now being employed with dignity and success. "Meditation isn't a substitute for standard medical treatment, but a *complement* to it." (p. 137)

The Nobel Laureate Pearl S. Buck in her essay on 'East and West' pertinently points out that: "There is nothing incomprehensible in the East or in the West. We are like men digging a tunnel through a mountain. We have begun at opposite ends but the goal is the same-human happiness. We ought to meet some where one of these days, and find that each faces the other's light." (Quoted in Arthur Christy's The Asian Legacy and American Life. p. 235)

Graf von Durckheim in his Jawaharlal Memorial Lecture delivered on 10th November 1974 in New Delhi on 'Eastern Influence on Western Spirituality' advances succinctly his understanding as follows:

...The discovery of the two poles in human being assumes a larger aspect if we realize that the symbols of Yin and Yang apply to the Asian and Western spirit. So the words, 'east' and 'west' do not only have a geographical meaning, but represent the two poles of life at work in each one of us. The difference between eastern and western traditions has to be understood in this – that in the eastern tradition the accent lies more on the Yin, and the western tradition more on the Yang. Yin means the more female character aiming at ultimate oneness; Yang, the more masculine character, which aims at and creates particular forms. Both trends exist in all men, and the time has come to bring about a conscious integration of the two poles all the world over. (Indian & Foreign Review, December 1, 1974, p. 18)

Rudyard Kipling, the Victorian poet, the poet of Empire, in his rhetorical and declamatory patriotic verse loudly prophesied:

> "O, East is East, and West is West
> And never the twain shall meet
> Till earth and sky stand presently
> At God's great judgement seat."

"Kipling long since dead, the Empire in retreat, and the Victorian ethos dethroned..." (Cox, p. 152) Kipling's prophesy now has no validity. It was more of his short-term arrogance rather than his vision of reality.

The October 13, 1996 issue of our local newspaper *The Spectrum* on page D-4 flashes a high-tech headline: "East and West meet in Cyberspace." From one end of the earth to the other, we are more alike than different. In our similarities, we share; in our differences, we complement each other.

I humbly and justifiably announce myself that I embody the synthesis of the East and the West. (I owe an apology for any imperfections, crudities, and generalizations contained in my presentation.)

OM OM OM

Works Cited

Barry, Thomas. 'Education in a Multicultural World'.

Approaches to the Oriental Classics: Asian Literature and Thought. Ed. Wm. Theodore de Bary. Morningside Heights, New York: Columbia University Press, 1959. 11-23.

Bowie, Theodore. East-West in Art: Patterns of Cultural & Aesthetic Relationships. Introduction Rudolf Wittkower. Bloomington: Indiana University P., 1966.

Browder, Sue. 'Relieving Chronic Pain without Drugs'. Reader's Digest. Pleasantville, N.Y.: The Reader's Digest Association, November 1996, 135-139.

Buck, Pearl S. 'Conclusion: East and West'. The Asian Legacy and American Life. Ed. Arthur E. Christy. New York: John Day Company, 1942, 231-235.

Carpenter, Frederick I. 'Eugene O'Neill, the Orient, and American Transcendentalism'. Transcendentalism and its Legacy. Eds. Myron Simm and Thornton H. Parsons. Ann Arbor: The University of Michigan P., 1966. Second Prtg. 1967.

Chan, Wing-Tsit. Tran. Introdn. & Notes. The Way of Lao Tzu. Indianapolis: Bobbs-Merrill Educational Publishing, 1963. Eleventh Printing 1978.

Christy, Arthur E. Ed. The Asian Legacy and American Life. New York: John Day Company, 1942.

The Orient in American Transcendentalism: A Study of Emerson, Thoreau, and Alcott. New York: Octagon Books, Inc., 1963. rpt.

Cox, Harvey. Turning East: The Promise and Peril of the New Orientalism. New York: Simon and Schuster, 1977.

Durckheim, Graf von. 'Eastern Influence on Western Spirituality' I. Indian and Foreign Review. December 1, 1974, 18-19.

Eck, Diana L. 'Religious America: Perspectives on Pluralism'. Unpublished article. Cambridge: Harvard University, 1996, 1-48.

Eliot, T.S. The Complete Poems and Plays, London: Faber & Faber, 1969.

Notes toward the Definition of Culture. London: Faber & Faber, 1948.

The Use of Poetry and the Use of Criticism. London: Faber & Faber, 1933.

Gulick, Sidney Lewis. The East and the West: A Study of their Psychicand Cultural Characteristics. Rutland, Vermont: Charles. E. Tuttle Company, Publishers. 1963

Horst Frenz, Ed. Asia and the Humanities: Papers Presented at the Second Conference on Oriental-Western Literary and Cultural Relations. Bloomington, Indiana U. Danville Illinois: Interstate Printers & Publishers, Inc., 1959.

Kaplan, Marty. 'Ambushed by Spirituality'. Time 24 June, 1996: 62.

Miller, Barbara Stoler, Trans. Introdn. Afterword. The Bhagavad Gita. New York: Bantam Books, 1986.

Nakamura, Hajime. Ways of Thinking of Eastern Peoples: India. China, Tibet, Japan. Rev. English trans. Ed. Philip P. Wiener. Honolulu: University of Hawaii P.

Pachori, S. S. 'Emerson's Essay on 'Illusions' and Hindu Maya'. Kyushu American Literature. 18, October 1977, 45-51.

Radhakrishnan, S. Eastern Religions and Western Thought. 1939. London: Oxford University Press, 1969.

Robinson, James A. Eugene O'Neill and Oriental Thought: A Divided Vision. Carbondale: Southern Illinois University P., 1982

Sri, P.S. T. S. Eliot, Vedanta and Buddhism. Vancouver: University of British Columbia Press, 1985.

Other Related Works of Interest

Braden, Charles S. 'The Novelist Discovers the Orient'. The Far Eastern Quarterly. 7, 1947, 165-175.

Chatterji-Gratry, Usha. 'India's Contribution to World Civilization'. India & Foreign Review, July 1976, 24-26.

Danto, Arthur C. Mysticism and Morality: Oriental Thought and Moral Philosophy. New York: Basic Books, Inc. Publishers, 1972.

Gue'non, Rene. East and West. Trans. William Massey. London, Luzac ~ Co., 1941.

Haas, William S. The Destiny of the Mind: East and West. New York: The Macmillan Company, 1956.

Jung, C. G. Psychology and Religion: West and East. Trans. R.F.C. Hull. Second edn. Bollingen Series XX. Princeton, NJ.: Princeton University P., 1969.

Miner, Earl. The Japanese Tradition in British and American Literature. Princeton, NJ.: Princeton University P, 1958.

Parsons, Howard L. Man East and West: Essays in East-West Philosophy. Amsterdam: B.R. Gruner, 1975.

Pope Jr., Harrison. The Road East: America's New Discovery of Eastern Wisdom. Boston: Beacon Press, 1974.
Radhakrishnan, S. Religion and Culture. New Delhi: Orient Paperbacks, 1968. 14th Reprint. 1989.

Said W. Edward. <u>Orientalism</u>. New York: Vintage Books, 1979. Afterword edn. 1994.

Thomas, Wendell. <u>Hinduism Invades America</u>. New York City: The Beacon Press, Inc., 1930.
Urquhart, W.S. <u>The Vedanta and Modern Thought</u>. London: Oxford University P., 1928.

Watts, Alan W. <u>Psychotherapy: East and West</u>. New York: Pantheon Books, 1961. Second Printing.

Thoreau and Emerson in India

Prologue

Both Thoreau and Emerson did not finally join Brahma after they had ceased their physical beings on the Edenic American soil. Despite their concerted efforts, they could not break the cycle of rebirths, for they were destined to complete expiation of sins of their previous births. And the ideal spot in the terrestrial world that would promote consummation of the much-desired oneness with the Over-Soul is India. Accordingly, the last reincarnation of Thoreau and Emerson was ordained to be the sanctified Indian soil. This was a noble and great move on the part of the Almighty God who had taken into consideration the sincerity of the two American transcendentalists as also their kinship with and penchant for the sacred scriptures of the Hindus.

Both Thoreau and Emerson are now Gandhi and Nehru respectively who are now in the exchanged roles of *Guru* and *Sishya.* They are also the dawn and the morning star of the emerging independent India. Likewise, they are the two sacred rivers – the Brown Gods – the Ganges and the Jamuna. The two erstwhile transcendentalists *rishis* are now the political seers and social sages.

Scene

At the confluence of the two sacred rivers, Allahabad, a city in north-eastern India.

Nehru scrupulously built a small sacred cottage, rather a hut, in the remote corner of the spacious, luscious green lawns of his palatial home, Anand Bhawan. The hut was palmyra and coconut dry leaves for its roof ably supported by bamboo, and mud walls heavily daubed with the sacred cow dung paste. In deference to the wishes of Mahatma Gandhi, Pandit Jawaharlal Nehru has made certain that the hut doesn't have electricity. Like the Sevagram hut, this one too has a three-by-eight-foot living room, which is furnished with a *charkha* (spinning wheel), a small writing table, a wastepaper basket, a straw mat, a board that Gandhiji could use as a prop for his back, and a limited stock of books – including the *Bhagawad Gita,* and *The Gospel of St. John,* and the *Koran.* A specially indented paperweight inscribed, "God is Love," is kept on the writing table. On one wall one can find a picture of Jesus, on another a motto: "When you are in the right, you can afford to keep your temper, and when you are in the wrong, you cannot afford to lose it." Apart from his minimal clothing – a loin cloth and a shawl – Gandhiji's worldly goods consist of a pocket watch to remind him constantly of the hour of India's independence, two food bowls, a water pitcher, several fountain pens, some stationery, and a pair of spectacles. The spectacles enabled him to see the invisible. Another major feature of Gandhiji's little hut, like his own at Sevagram, is an enormous window that dominates the entrance-symbolically suggesting and inviting the whole population to look in on him.

Time

It is the January of the mid-1940s at about seven o'clock in the morning. Gandhiji had recently arrived from Wardha, Sevagram, on a special mission to Allahabad in response to a longstanding invitation from Nehru in order to conduct their confabulations. Their intention is to devote their time on urgent national matters since their correspondence has failed to iron out their differences on various organizational, institutional, national, international, and personal matters. Being the first day of their frank and heart-to-heart talks, they tend to be nostalgic, vague, and flippant.

Identification

'Bapu' is the endearing salutation that Nehru uses for Gandhi.

Jawahar is the first name of Nehru

Gandhi slowly begins to remember his previous birth, whereas, Nehr doesn't remember his. But, unwittingly, he keeps making references to Emerson; sometimes he echoes Emerson's ideas and occasionally quotes him.

A Clause

I invoke the Coleridgean dictum of 'willing suspension of disbelief that constitutes...' *The sin qua non* of imaginary dialogs.

Dialog

Immediately after dawn, Nehru, majestically and radiantly, proceeds to Gandhiji's cottage to pay his respects. Gandhiji, in his inimitable style, doesn't particularly pay attention to the expected arrival of Nehru. He has just completed the readings from *Bhagawad Gita,* the *Holy Bible,* and the sacred *Koran,* and has begun his simple breakfast of fruits and goats-milk. Rituals and breakfast over, Gandhi waves to Nehru.

Gandhi:	Hare Ram! How are you, Jawahar? Oh! You have the youthful vigor in you. Perhaps, you owe it to the *Sirshasan* that you perform regularly.
Nehru:	Yes, Bapu. I'm sure you are happy with the replica of your Sevagram cottage. I'm a little struck at your insistence on the large window for this small structure.
Gandhi:	You know for certain I wish to meet the facts of life face-to-face. My hut represents the common man of India – the farmer – and the window allows me to be constantly aware of and in touch with the mass of Indian peasants

	who lead lives of quiet desperation. It is strictly from this point of view that I've reduced my life to its lowest terms. And 'I've conceived my mission to be that of a knight-errant wandering everywhere to deliver people from difficult situations. My humble occupation, as was known for certain, is to show people how they can solve their own difficulties'.
Nehru:	As Emerson said, "The glory of the farmer is that, in the division of labors, it is his part to create. He stands close to nature, but I am fascinated by Emerson's writings, particularly because they have such a stunning validity to India and Indian people; and they fit into the oriental frame exquisitely.
Gandhi:	The window that you have questioned about has another meaningful suggestion. It refers to our catholic approach to life – our desire to imbibe spirit from outside influences. The great American transcendentalist and contemporary of Emerson, Thoreau, very aptly, said... "The most interesting dwellings in this country... are the most unpretending, humble log huts and cottages of the poor commonly..." And these belong to the poor fanners and the labor class.
Nehru:	Though I differ with your views, Bapu, I do agree that it is from the farmer 'that the health and power, moral and intellectual, of the cities come'. Farmer is the continuous benefactor. But, you seem to imply that Anand Bhawan is not an interesting dwelling.
Gandhi:	Jawahar, palaces and temples are the luxury of the princes; and whatever cannot be shared with the masses is taboo to me. Service of the poor has been my heart's desire and it has

	always thrown me amongst them. I may sound idealistic in my attitude, but my work will be finished once I succeed in carrying conviction to the human family, that every man or woman is the guardian of his or her self-respect and liberty.
Nehru:	What you've said is close to the spirit of democracy with its broad objectives related to human welfare and human development, providing opportunity to every human being to develop to the fullest measure possible. Perhaps, this is a synthesis of capitalism and communism. Emerson strongly felt that democracy was eminently suitable for America, because, according to him, the religious enticement of his times accorded better with it.
Gandhi:	How come, Jawahar, you are either quoting or echoing Emerson?
Nehru:	Bapu, you too seem to be quoting Emerson's contemporary, Thoreau? I have in *The Discovery of India* quoted at length Emerson, and I'm fresh with my reading of his works and essays like 'The American Scholar', 'Self-Reliance', 'Education', 'Politics', *Nature,* and so forth.
Gandhi:	Jawahar, do you believe in the Hindu concept of rebirth?
Nehru:	Why do you ask about it, Bapu?
Gandhi:	You wouldn't, as usual, believe if I say I seemed to have imbibed the spirit of Thoreau as regards my simplicity in life, thought, attitudes, and habits. Would you?
Nehru:	I do not yet understand any connection between the concept of rebirth and your references to Thoreau.
Gandhi:	I might sound incredible as also authoritarian if I revealed the strange dream I dreamt last

	night. It wasn't merely a fantasy, but was a total unfolding of my past life – rather my previous birth.
Nehru:	You seem to be treading into Freudian realms.
Gandhi:	On the contrary, I am immersed in the bracing waters of Gita, the Veda, as also the other holy scriptures. And I have faith in the Hindu interpretation of dreams. Are you aware of Emerson's influence on you?
Nehru:	I am puzzled, Bapu.
Gandhi:	Let me get back to the dream, Jawahar. So far, we have touched the subject only tangentially. According to the dream, in our previous birth we had our abodes not on the banks of the sacred Indian rivers but on the American soil. I had set up my hut on the shores of Walden pond where peace used to come to me, dropping slow. I was Thoreau and you were Emerson while Gurudev Tagore, perhaps, was Walt Whitman, though both of them were alive at the same time. You were my guru then. Now I am your guru. In a way, our previous roles of teacher-disciple are reversed in the present birth, though not totally.
Nehru:	I don't deny my interest in Emerson. But this has no relationship to what you have said.
Gandhi:	In my previous birth, I had my own cottage similar to the one I've erected at Sevagram. I led the same austere and economical life that I'm now leading. And I fought for the same ideals that I am now fighting for. I had read the same scriptures of different religions of the world that I'm now reading and assimilating
Nehru:	I can't find or realize any rationale or logic in what you have enumerated, Bapu.

From the beginning, my approach to life's problems has been more or less scientific. Essentially, I am interested in this world, in this life, not in some other world, or past or future life. Whether there is such a thing as a soul, or whether there is a survival after death or not, I do not know. Perhaps, these questions are important, but they do not trouble me in the least. I still am vague in my answer to your question. I would say yes and no. Perhaps my western education and background in science—'the voices of my education' – tells me that I should not subscribe to the Hindu concept of rebirth. But the environment in which I have grown up takes the soul (or rather the atma) and a future life, the Karma theory of cause and effect, and reincarnation for granted. I have been affected by this traditional, orthodox Hindu pull and so, in a sense, I am favorably disposed to those assumptions. "There might be a soul which survives the physical death of the body, and a theory of cause and effect governing life's actions seems reasonable, though it leads to obvious difficulties when one thinks of the ultimate cause, presuming a soul. There appears to be some logic also in the theory of reincarnation." But I do not believe in any of these or other theories and assumptions as a matter of religious faith. They are first intellectual speculations in an unknown region about which we know next to nothing. "Spiritualism with its séances and so-called manifestations of spirits and the like has always seemed to me a rather absurd and impertinent way of investigating psychic phenomena and the mysteries of the

	afterlife." It is a bourne from which no traveler returns.
Gandhi:	There isn't any organic thought in you, Jawahar. You seem to be inconsistent and vague.
Nehru:	Foolish consistency is the hallmark of little minds, while inconsistency is an indication of the developing mind as also maturity.
Gandhi:	You are misquoting Emerson. I am myself not at all concerned with appearing to be consistent. I might well endorse my guru's saying that 'Foolish consistency is the hobgoblin of little minds'. There is, I fancy, a method in my inconsistencies. "In my opinion, there is a consistency running through my seeming inconsistencies, as in nature, there is unity running through seeming diversity." In my pursuit after truth, I have discarded many ideas and learnt many new things. I am old, but I have no feeling that I have ceased to grow inwardly. What I am concerned with is my readiness to obey the call of truth, my God, from moment to moment. "My aim is not to be consistent with my previous statements on a given question, but to be consistent with truth." This enables me to grow from truth to truth.
Nehru:	Bapuji, then, do you mean to suggest that it is blasphemous if I did not blindly accept and acquiesce in the theory? What the mysterious is, I do not know. I do not call it God because God has come to mean much that I do not believe in. The Vedanta and other similar approaches frighten me with their vague, formless incursions into infinity. Some kind of ethical approach to life appeals to me strongly, though it is well-nigh difficult for

	me to justify it logically. Here I respond to my own intuition.
Gandhi:	Strange, Jawahar! In your previous birth, you believed in God, the Over-Soul, and came out with the dictum that the Kingdom of God was within every individual and that individual conscience should have the final authority. You were even mystical in as much as you believed that the individual would transcend the limits of his individuality and feel himself part of the whole in order to share omniscience of God, or the Over-Soul. And in tune with our own Hindu philosophy, you had affirmed that the soul would go beyond the body to achieve identification with God. You did celebrate this aspect of unity in diversity in your poem 'Brahma'.
Nehru:	I am confounded with what you have so cogently and authoritatively said. "Whether we believe in God or not, it is impossible not to believe in something, whether we call it a creative life-giving force or vital energy inherent in matter which gives it its capacity for self-movement and change and growth, or by some other name, something that is real, though elusive, as life is real when contrasted with death." I do think that life cut off completely from the soil will ultimately wither away. Be that as it may, I am too much of an individualist and a believer in personal freedom to excessive regimentation imposed by books of religion. Whatever gods there may be, there is something godlike in man; as there is something of a devil in man. "The real problems for me remain problems of individual and social life, of harmonious living, of a proper balancing of an individual's inner and outer life, an

	adjustment of the relations between individuals and between groups, of continuous becoming something better and higher of social development, of the ceaseless adventure of the man. In the solution of these problems, the way of observation and precise knowledge and deliberate reasoning, according to the methods of science, must be followed." This method may not always be applicable in our quest for truth, for art and poetry and certain psychic experiences perhaps belong to an inexplicable realm of things and elude the analytical and objective methods of science. Let us, therefore, not rule out intuition and other methods of sensing truth and reality.
Gandhi:	(He picks up a glass of water and drinks.) My faith is in God, and I won't convince you by argument. This is what I had said in my letter to you about ten years ago. "I cannot leave religion and therefore Hinduism. I love Christianity, Islam, and many other faiths through Hinduism." But religion is after all a matter for each individual and then too a matter of the heart...
Nehru:	But dogmas irritate me, Bapu. What impresses me is the growth of mind and spirit of man. Many Hindus look upon Vedas as revealed scripture. This seems to be peculiarly ridiculous. Certainly, I do endorse the views of Gurudev Tagore in his attack on your public statement, about eleven years ago, after the terrible earthquake in Bihar. You had asserted that calamity was 'a divine chastisement sent by God' for the sin of untouchability. By that assertion, you seemed to have strengthened the elements of

	unreason. This is a fundamental source of all the blind powers that drive us against freedom and self-respect.
Gandhi:	I cannot prove the connection of the sin of untouchability, which is like slavery in America, the one that I was concerned with when I was Thoreau – with the Bihar visitation. But I instinctively felt the connection. "Visitations like droughts, floods, earthquakes and the like, though they seem to have only physical origins, are, for me, somehow connected with man's morals. With me, the connection between cosmic phenomena.
Nehru:	Bapu, this is a staggering explanation. Anything opposed to the scientific outlook would be difficult to imagine.
Gandhi:	Oh! Jawahar, how much you are different from your previous birth. As in my previous birth, I am a born protestant. As Thoreau, I stood for abolition of slavery and raised my voice against the inhuman and shameful treatment of the Indians now. I stand for abolition of untouchability. As in America in the nineteenth century, I 'signed off' from an unjust state and refused to pay my town tax; as a consequence, I was forced to spend a night in jail. In the wake of that experience, I wrote an electric essay, 'Civil Disobedience'. Now, as an Indian in the twentieth century, I have implemented the same principle of civil disobedience in South Africa. I have, since then, continued to practice it for nobler ends – our conscientious objection to the unethical and unjust political institutions of the British rule and social structures like untouchability. Like Thoreau, one should use disobedience, Satyagraha, as a weapon only, so long as it is

	used in the right spirit-that of the man who tries by nonviolence to shame his opponent into a recognition of the truth. To me, nonviolence, Ahimsa, is a means to an end because I am concerned with the moral purity of the program. Let me also refresh your memory about the passage that I had written in Hind Swaraj which is related to the doctrine of Passive Resistance: Passive Resistance is a method of securing rights by personal suffering; it is the reverse of resistance by arms. When I refuse to do a thing that is repugnant of my conscience, I use soul-force... If I do not obey the law, and accept the penalty for its breach, I use soul-force. It involves sacrifice of self...
Nehru:	I, on the other hand, look for the result – the destruction of the power of the British government in India. I don't approve of your religious and sentimental approach to a political question.
Gandhi:	Jawahar, I think we have strayed away from the future course of action that we need to adopt after we attain independence. The independent India should aim at a society that would be like 'Ram Rajya' where none should have grievances against the state.
Nehru:	I am one with you, Bapu. The state should not be superior to the citizen. Emerson too believed that man should free himself from the compulsions of political authority and of economic necessity, though it is impractical to endorse his view that man must surrender his individual will and intellect and act in accordance with the dictates of the instincts of his soul. It should, however, be our endeavor to have less government, fewer

	laws, and less.-confided power. We would also, in accordance with the views of Emerson which are relevant to us today, fix the highest end of the government to be the culture of men. "For if men can be educated, the institutions will share their improvement and the moral sentiment will write the law of the land." There has to be finally a balance, an attempt at harmony between the externals and the significance of the inner life of man. "In our individual lives also, we have to discover a balance between the body and the spirit, and between man as part of nature and man as part of society."
Gandhi:	Yes, Jawahar. We ought to inculcate also a spirit of nationalism among our countrymen who are still living in isolated communities as loners.
Nehru:	At any rate, the world of Emerson's time has changed. Now that old barriers are breaking down, life becomes more international. But the internationalism has to grow out of national cultures, and it can have meaningful relevance on the basis of freedom and equality and true internationalism. Bapu, let me frankly admit that in me, there is still a western attitude of life. Maybe, I ought to cut the occidental adventitious roots lest I should be an alien sapling on my own soil.
Gandhi:	Do you now understand the further significance of the gigantic window in my hut? "It was India's way in the past to welcome and absorb other cultures. That is more vital today, for we march to the one world of tomorrow where national barriers will be lost in the international entity of the human race." The window is on the world, on India, and for the Indian peasant.

Nehru:	There is a kisan group waiting for your darshan. I shall join you after your evening prayers. (Nehru leaves Gandhiji's hut reciting the following lines.)

One's self I sing, a simple separate person,
Yet utter the word Brahma

The Concept of Evolution/Progression: Past, Present, and Future in Whitman's 'Passage to India'

Without beginning and without end, without any base and pediment, (Whitman's poetry) sweeps past forever, like a wind that is forever in passage, and unchainable.

— D. H. Lawrence

Neither road was yet to be taken, nor path was yet to be charted; neither was he to be chained by his meridian middle age, nor was he to be confined to geographical territories! Having sung the song of himself and of America, Walt Whitman was eventually ready to embark on a long voyage – beyond the expanse of America – 'with his soul as a companion' (Marinacci 268). And that journey was to materialize in his bold and ambitious poem 'Passage to India', 'the verse counterpart of *Democratic Vistas*' (Kaplan 318). Whitman's transcendental mind was restlessly eager for a 'passionate sense of the oneness of multiplicity' (Trilling 22), the unity in diversity, the Brahman, having crossed Brooklyn ferry.

> Darest thou now soul,
> Walk out with me toward the unknown region,
> Where neither ground is for the feet nor any path to follow.

The reader cannot afford to ignore background in coming to appreciate 'Passage to India'. The results of deflections from war, paralysis, neglect, and lowered spiritual vitality of the postwar period disabled Whitman from praising the body's physiognomy from 'tip to toe' and singing the 'Song of Myself', having lost the physical exuberance – gloriously celebrated as the 'now', the 'present' in *Leaves of Grass* – Whitman now became a specialist in the soul – rhapsodically sung as the hopeful 'future'. The 'present' to Whitman was significant and relevant only in terms of the 'future'; and the present earthly career seemed only preparatory for an afterlife – the life beyond the physical. "The personality of mortal life is most important with reference to the immortal, the unknown, the spiritual, the only permanently real, which as the ocean waits for and receives the rivers, waits for us each and all," Whitman wrote in *Democratic Vistas.*

James E. Miller traces the relationship between the poem and the related prose document: "Like *Democratic Vistas,* this poem called on America to venture beyond material achievement into the realm of spirit, to sail out daringly into the 'Seas of God'" (Introduction xxix). The fact that Whitman printed the poem 'Passage to India' separately in an annex to the fifth edition of *Leaves of Grass* (1871-1872) is a definite justification of this declaration. Though by incorporating 'Passage to India' poems into the main body of the seventh edition of *Leaves of Grass* (1881), Whitman finally accomplished that structure which had been for a life-time in evolution – the *Leaves of Grass* was in evolution from the first edition in 1855 and the 'death-bed edition' of 1891-1892. 'Passage to India' embodies a separate vigorous program – the program of 'Song of Spirit'. The whole group of 'Passage to India' poems (the chief title in a group of seventy-three poems), according to Gay Wilson Allen and Charles T. Davis 'was intended to be nucleus of a second volume, spiritual poems to balance and complete the more material poems in *Leaves of Grass.* Illness in 1873 prevented Whitman from achieving this ambition." (Allen and Davis 233)

It is thus evident that Whitman wanted to make 'Passage to India' a definite epoch in his poetic evolution-the end of the materialistic or nonspiritual *Leaves of Grass* and the beginning of a new spiritual cycle. Roger Asselineau affirms that 'from the beginning, he [Whitman] knew where he was going and what he wanted, what great themes he was going to treat: the body, then the spiritual life, and then, by a natural progression, death and immortality, and finally, man no longer alone but in society' (Asselineau 938). Against this background of Whitman's physical malaise and vigorous poetic programs, the following entry dated 15th May 1888 in 'Conversations with Traubel' is immensely valuable and serves as a guide to the critical reader to appreciate the poem in the context of the spirit in which it was written:

A younger man and disciple, Horace Traubel, became a kind of Boswell to Whitman in his old age, paying him extended visits and holding long conversations with him. He scrupulously recorded every detail. In 1906, he began publication of a series of large volumes under the title *With Walt Whitman in Camden*, containing verbatim all of his copious notes about his visits with Good Gray Poet. (Miller 36-37)

Whitman, referring to 'Passage to India':

There's more of me, the essential ultimate me, in that than in any of the poems. There is no philosophy, consistent or inconsistent, in that poem – but the burden of it is evolution – the one thing escaping the other – the unfolding of cosmic purposes. (Traubel 156-57)

My analysis of the poem substantiates Whitman's affirmation of the concept of spiritual evolution. For example, in appreciation of 'Passage to India', John Lovell, Jr., repudiates Whitman's own view of the poem:

Perhaps Whitman was exaggerating when in 1888 he declared that 'Passage to India' contained more of himself than had any other poem. Perhaps not... that it did not get into *Leaves of Grass* until 1881 suggests that he considered it a bold, separate declaration of his much-

72

declared independence of spirit... that it was three different poems rolled into one, yet essentially unified, provokes curiosity about Whitman's successful brooding process at this time. (132)

On the other hand, Richard Chase is more than unjust in his summary treatment of the poem; he considers it a 'piece'. It does 'not appeal to [him] very much... because Whitman has given up poetry and become a speechmaker'. In support of his thesis, Chase quotes the following lines from the poem.

The Past – the dark unfathom'd retrospect!
The teeming gulf – the sleepers and the shadows!
The past – the infinite greatness of the past!

These lines are not those of a 'speechmaker'; they, on the other hand, suggest the urgency of Whitman's concern for realization of the past in terms of the present. Fuller appreciation of 'Passage to India' can be had if the reader approaches from the angle of the total vision of 'evolution' as revealed in the treatment of past, present, and future.

Whitman begins his poem by 'singing the great achievements of the present'. The 'modern wonders' (1.4) are the Suez Canal in the Old World, the 'mighty railroad' in the New World, and the Atlantic Cable with its 'eloquent gentle wires'. The achievements of the present of which the poet sings are the contemporary achievements of spanning the globe and bringing the heretofore separated worlds together. The three geographical entities, recognized by Whitman with the three significant eras of history, are eventually linked. These engineering feats and scientific and technological advancements are an indication of the materialistic progress in the present; the poet now reflects on the present as an offshoot of the past:

The past – the infinite greatness of the past!
For what is the present after all but a growth out of the past!

To Whitman, the present does not exist in a vacuum; it is a growth from out of the stems of the past. Thus, both past and present are part of the evolutionary process. Section-I of the poem concludes with a direct and definite assertion of Whitman's belief in spiritual progress:

As a projectile form'd, impell'd, passing a certain line, still keeps on, So the present, utterly form'd, impell'd by the past.

(The terms 'form'd', 'impell'd' are past tense; 'passing' is both present and present continuous; and 'still keeps on' is future tense.)

Both the concepts of time and of the growth of humankind as evolutionary progression are interfused in the image of projectile. It is 'God's purpose from the first' that there should be progression in terms of gradual development, not in a disorganized and chaotic manner, but in a systematic form. This process of evolution from plant to animal to human is evocatively evidenced in the last section of the poem, while future development or progression to a higher stage lies in spiritual growth.

Have we not stood here like trees in the ground long enough?
Have we not grovel'd here long enough, eating and drinking like mere brutes?
Have we not darken'd and dazed ourselves with hooks long enough?

These lines even reassert the Darwinian theory of evolution. The lower stage of brute man has ascended to the level of an intelligent, scholarly, and creative being and aims at ascending further into a spiritual being. All the accomplishments and efforts in the present are ultimately directed to reaching the still-higher stage that can be realized only in the future. The present 'strong light works of engineers' are not for immediate materialistic benefits – 'not for trade or transportation only' – but for the sake of the soul, 'in God's name, and for the sake of soul'. This is the future that Whitman seeks fervently in the poem. And to Whitman the route to the spiritual lies through the material. "Projecting his intuition into the future, the poet evokes the millennium, when not only the continents shall be spanned and joined by physical means, but all peoples of the globe shall likewise be linked together by love and understanding." (Allen 429).

The earth to be spann'd, connected by network,
The races, neighbors, to marry and be given in marriage,
The oceans to be cross'd, the distant brought near,
The lands to be welded together.

Thus, Whitman through a progressive process apprehends physical unity on the earth – all the diversities are dismantled, distances conquered, and unity accomplished. His endless enumerations and catalogs always move toward the hoped – for unity. In 'Crossing Brooklyn Ferry', all the 'dumb, beautiful ministers' – the river, the 'scallop-edg'd waves', the clouds, the 'masts of Manahattan', and the 'beautiful hills of Brooklyn' finally merge into unity. Richard P. Adams aptly remarks that: 'Passage to India' expresses 'the final unity toward which the assimilation of diverse experience is supposed to lead' – "its scope is universal. Beginning in that present moment with which Thoreau and Emerson were *so* much fascinated, it integrates the present with the past and future in a way that neither Emerson nor Thoreau was ever quite able to match". (Adams 111-49).

"Complete and final unity can be accomplished only in the future. The process of evolution ultimately leads back to the Creator, and God is conceived as essentially identical with the principle of organization in the universe. The technological achievements of engineers, architects, machinists, captains, voyagers, and explorers actually lead humankind to the understanding and realization of its past, to the people and lands ('the myths Asiatic', 'the primitive fables'), where people were engaged in religious and spiritual pursuits and quests of the human soul. It is in this context that India functions as a vital symbol in the poem. India is not only a continent, the historical cradle of humanity and of religion and of all great dreams for the race; it is also a symbol of spirituality and the ultimate meaning of existence." (Allen 429). So Whitman in his old age prompts his soul to sail along toward the East, 'to primal thought to realms of budding Bibles', and to the shores of soul-oriented Hinduism and Buddhism.

O soul, repressless, I with thee and thou with me,
Thy circumnavigation of the world begin,
Of man, the voyage of his mind's return
To reason's early paradise,
Back, back to wisdom's birth, to innocent intuitions,
Again with fair creation.

This is the significance of the past in the poem. The achievements of the present have enabled the poet to have an awareness of the significance of the past, and he can now hope for the swift journey of the soul into the future.

Nature and Man shall be disjoin'd and diffused no more,
The true son of God shall absolutely fuse them
And there is no need for further evolution. And there will be no more
Wandering, yearning, curious, with restless explorations,
With questionings, baffled, formless, feverish, with never-happy hearts.

Finally, the 'restless explorations' are justified.

Henry S. Canby asserts that the poem 'was written to spiritualize progress through glorifying the age of the machine and triumphant science' (339). The spiritual progress of humankind is the pinnacle of evolution that Whitman refers to in his conversations with Traubel; and this is the cycle of progress which has its beginnings in the past, continuation in the present, and progress in the future. Undoubtedly, the future is contained in the line 'Passage to more than India' – perhaps even beyond the spiritual.

Despite his repudiation of Whitman's own assertion of the theme of the poem, John Lovell, Jr., concludes that 'Passage to India', apart from being a chart of progressive civilization, 'indicates the motive power of progress, man's insatiable passion for the next higher stage, and the reasons for the illimitability of that power, the constant urging from God' (141). Emerson in his essay 'The Poet' alludes to the power of progress and the innate urge and motivation to reach the next higher stage, as *metamorphosis.* This is fundamental in nature: "Within the form of every creature is a force impelling it to ascend into a higher form... nature has a higher end." (Emerson 330-31)

Perhaps Whitman's conception of evolution radiates this spirit of a higher form of man – the spiritual fulfillment of humankind.

The evolutionary emergence of life is also projected in the recurring image of the 'sea' in the poem.

> Sail forth – steer for the deep waters only,
> Reckless of soul, exploring, I with thee, and thou
> with me,
> For we are bound where mariner has not yet dared
> to go.

The aesthetic use of 'water' and 'sea' images is designed to suggest that water is normally associated with birth, and birth is part of evolution. Secondly, the imagery of 'flowing' connotes evolution in that it encompasses all three stages – past, present, and future. Allen affirms that 'the imagery and rhythms of 'flowing' are always prominent in Whitman's poetry when he treats the subject of death (as in 'The Sleepers', 'Out of the Cradle Endlessly Rocking', the latter part of 'When Lilacs Last...'), and the flowing motif is very effective in some lines' (Allen 209-10) in 'Passage to India' – 'lave me all over, *I* Bathe me of God'. In Whitman's view, death is birth, a rebirth – an entry into the spiritual world; perhaps this is the last stage of the progress of evolution. Thus, water in directional motion like 'river Euphrates flowing', the 'streams' of the Indus and Ganges and their 'affluents' suggest movement and progression, while the ocean itself stands for the evolutionary source of all life – both birth and death.

Whitman's physical decline led to his spiritual ascension – the logical organic process of growth in terms of knowledge, awareness, and wisdom. *Leaves of Grass* – particularly 'Song of Myself' and 'Passage to India' – symbolically represents birth and growth. Thus, even in Whitman's poetic career there is an evolutionary progression from physical to spiritual: 'truths', 'facts', and 'the spirit'. As with Emerson, so with Whitman: one can be aware of universality by simple observation of the process of things, the pattern of life, the birth and death, and the appearance and disappearance of all phenomena. This could lead one to the inference that this ascending pattern must somehow be sustained by a central dynamic principle. "Hence it is that Whitman found no difficulty in weaving evolutionary theory into the view of the world." (Jones 89) The thrust or the burden of the poem, as Whitman asserts, is: "Evolution – the one thing escaping the other – the unfolding of cosmic purposes'. Startling though it was to the popular mind of late nineteenth-century America, 'to men of culture the idea of evolution... was hardly new. A man like Whitman, for example, could write of 'this old theory, evolution, as broach'd anew, trebled, with indeed all devouring claims by Darwin'." (Hofstadter 14)

'Passage to India' is a joyous poem of celebration that charts humankind's evolutionary growth – before 'the world of 1492' and on to progress; it is a minor epic that sings gloriously about human infinitude. "Despite the title, this poem is not so Vedantic as 'Song of Myself', but perhaps it was more prophetic than we Westerners had realized." (Allen, Foreword to *Vedantic Mysticism* ix)

Note

I started typing this paper on March 26, 1992, the day of Whitman's Hundredth Death Anniversary.

Works Cited

Adams, Richard P. 'Whitman: A Brief Revaluation'. *Tulane Studies in English* 5 (1955): 111-49.

Allen, Gay Wilson. 'Foreword' to V. K. Chari's *Whitman in the Light of Vedantic Mysticism.* Lincoln: U of Nebraska P, 1964.

A Reader's Guide to Walt Whitman. New York: Farrar, 1970.

The Solitary Singer: A Critical Biography of Walt Whitman. New York: Macmillan, 1955.

Asselineau, Roger. 'The 'Plan' for *Leaves of Grass* from *The Evolution of Walt Whitman: The Creation of Personality.* Ed. Sculley Bradley and Harold W Blodgett. New York: Norton, 1973.

Canby, Henry S. *Walt Whitman, an American.* Boston: Miffiin, 1943. Chase, Richard. *Walt Whitman Reconsidered.* New York: Sloane, 1955.

Emerson, Ralph Waldo. *The Complete Essays and Other Writings.* Modern Library College edition. New York: Random House, 1950.

Hofstadter, Richard. *Social Darwinism in American Thought.* Rev. ed. Boston: Beacon, 1955.

Jones, Howard Mumford. 'The Cosmic Optimism of Walt Whitman'. *Belief and Disbelief in American Literature.* Chicago: U of Chicago P, 1967.

Kaplan, Justin. *Walt Whitman: A Life.* New York: Simon and Schuster, 1980.

Lovell, John, Jr. Appreciating Whitman: 'Passage to India'. *Modern Language Quarterly* 21.2 (June 1960): 131-41.

Marinacci, Barbara. *O Wondrous Singer! An Introduction to Walt Whitman.* New York: Dodd, 1970.

Miller, James E., Jr. *Walt Whitman.* Twayne Series. New York: Twayne, 1962.

Traubel, Horace. *With Walt Whitman in Camden,* Boston: Small Maynard, 1906 Trilling, Lionel. *The Liberal Imagination.* New York: Doubleday, 1954. Whitman, Walt. *Complete Poetry and Selected Prose.* Ed. James E. Miller, Jr. Boston: Houghton Mifflin, 1959.

Indian Caste System – Applicability to Us Indians in North America

Having voluntarily uprooted ourselves from the soil of India along with the adventitious root of social values and taboos of Indian society, we are, I believe, objectively inclined to examine, evaluate, and endorse all that we instinctively accepted. What we ignorantly practiced in the past, especially the tenets of caste system, has assumed a certain disturbing vitality in the midst of western culture, society, and religions. As we are all aware, we are continually questioned by our neighbors and colleagues about the caste system that has ironically defied pat answers.

All thinking and intelligent Indians in America, it is presumed and believed, recognize that the Hindu caste system has tended to be self-destructive. It has aroused more passion, for and against, more bitterness, more political wrangling in the post-independent Indian than any other aspect of Hinduism, including the "sacred cow" issue and the Babri Masjid-Ayodhya temple tension. (It is irrelevant here to go into the historical factors, racial issues, and religious as well as social origins of the caste system.)

Most of us in North America recognize that the caste system seems an anachronism in the twentieth century, significantly so because economic security has given us strength. Moreover, we live in a society that stresses the value of self-reliance, individuality, and dignity of labor rather than inequalities and inexplicable abominations. Back in India, in a general historical sense, the caste system knit the Hindu society together. In fact, the system provided coherence and order.

And without the sanction and endorsement of religion among multi-racial people for whom cultural practices, social customs, politics, and religion were inextricably linked (as they were for Mahatma Gandhi)—the strength of the system lay in it being thought of by Hindus as part of the religion, thus making it sacred, its strict observance inviolable—the system of caste might have slowly withered and died. While the esurient politicians in the post-colonial and post-independent India have desperately tried to give a political chlorophyll to the caste system, yet historically, religion helped sustain the caste system from being eroded by or subjected to destruction by outside hostile winds and forces.

Neither morality nor human behavior can be legislated. Similarly, caste system cannot be pulled from its deeply entrenched soil. We all know it is an excrescence and and an impediment to individual and society's progress. Mahatma Gandhi genuinely wanted to reform the system as such. Fundamentally, we thought it was sound and still essential. But he was adamantly opposed to Hindus perpetuating the diabolical custom of regarding their fellowmen as 'untouchable'. As we all know, he fought valiantly against the practice of 'untouchability', which is strongest in South India, to his dying day.

What was applicable to us while we were in India may not be and need not be applicable to us here in North America unless we want to employ the deleterious effects of caste system for our political aggrandizement the way that is exercised in Indian political arena. After all, the use of caste system in North America can only be confined to Indian associations which are by definition essentially created and promoted for cultural cohesion. Even then, American democratic traditions do not admit nor tolerate the narrow caste prejudices of Indian social makeup to infiltrate American political, social, and cultural institutions. Consequently, the caste system may be irreverently drafted only into the Indian associations, politics, as manifested in the recent divisions in the TANA, resulting in the formation of the new Chicago group. (I am geographically isolated from the politics of various Indian associations of major American cities. A Blissful isolation it is!)

Let us also not disavow that our caste-consciousness has perhaps conditioned us to be extremely prejudiced in our dealing with fellow Indian-Americans; we tend to, sometimes unconsciously, press or exert our superior or inferior economic, social, cultural, and caste status, leading to perpetuation of the typical Indian petty-mindedness can be easily discarded by simply declaring that it is anti-social? We need a moral declaration of independence and an individual effort to overcome the restricting influence of caste system. We cannot possibly import everything Indian to satisfy our ego and cultural and social craving—we have sponsored our brothers and sisters and parents; we have established Indian grocery and jewelry stores; we have built temples in America; we have periodically invited musicians, dancers, and movie stars; we have even sponsored visits of Indian politicians and sung songs of sycophancy; we have fancifully and elaborately conditioned our homes with Indian décor, exhibited extravagantly our newly acquired material affluence; we have thrown lavish parties to impress our fellow Indian-Americans and Indian visitors.

And now it seems our craving for Indianness in North America hasn't been satiated yet. So, we are slowly embarking on the might project of importing the politically motivated Indian caste system into America! Why? To satisfy our blunted taste buds? To perpetuate prejudices?

Indian caste system is undoubtedly inapplicable to Indians in North America. Why should it even be applied? To start political parties? To perpetuate divisiveness? To demonstrate superiority? To create tensions? These are not rhetorical fragmentary questions.

If we are intending to build or promote a new Indian-American society, then are we not to have an enlightened approach, recognizing the adverse consequences of ignorant and blind following of casteism? Are our Indian associations created and nurtured meant to transplant the worn out roots of casteism on the virgin soil of America? Let us remind ourselves that the 19th-century bard of America Walt Whitman gloriously rhapsodized over "Passage O soul to India." But the 20th-century Indian immigrants seemed to have left behind spiritualism and came with the 'bag and baggage' of casteism.

Yes, caste is probably the most significant influence upon individual and collective behavior, according to the Hindu traditions. We all know 'caste' certainly does not enter celebration of 'Sankranthi', 'Ugadi', 'Ram Navami', 'Deepavali'; caste does not permeate 'kirtanas' of Tyagaraja and Annamacharyulu; caste does not prevent mixed audiences in theaters or 'sabhas'. So, where does caste enter? In politics or in social intercourse? Or in contracting marriages. But we cannot eliminate caste consciousness among Indian-Americans, especially in matrimonial alliances. (Let us look at the matrimonial page of March 92 issue of TANA Patrika: 'Niyogi Brahmin', 'Naidu', 'kamma', 'Reddy', 'vaisya', etc. Can we legislate that henceforth no such caste or sub-caste appellation would be used?

We may endeavor to have a planned process of adaptation to the needs, demands, and possibilities of the present that could dismantle the harsher, rigid, restrictive destructive components of the caste system while preserving its advantages of order and cohesion. The second-generation Indian-Americans are to a great extent growing up well-nigh oblivious to caste distinctions. Yet we the mature and intelligent adults are demonstrating our prejudices. Are our associations in America the battlefield "where ignorant armies clash by night"? (Matthew Arnold, "Dover Beach")

What we in North America need is not proclamation declaring that observance of caste system will not be tolerated. What we need, however, is to infuse a spirit of understanding, flexibility, tolerance, mutual respect, nonrancourness, nondivisiveness into our much misused, misinterpreted, misunderstood, misguided caste system. After all, we have adapted ourselves to the norms of our adopted society. Now let us adapt caste system beneficially to our needs.

Our transplanted roots in virgin soil require American water and nutrients!

***

(This essay won First Prize in the Adult Essay Writing competition held by the Telugu Association of North America in 1992; published in Tana Patrika, August 1992)

Poems

Sacred and Actual Places

In his life and in his writings, S. S. Moorty creates a special kind of bridge; and this collection of his poems will allow many readers to share an experience that his friends and students have cherished, the encounter with a thoroughly American scholar who also carries, lightly and with grace, a rich intellectual and spiritual background based on his native India and his flourishing career in America.

In his poem 'Who Am I?', this 'composite' author allows us to glimpse the many strands that make the distinctive flavor of a Moorty encounter: a catalog of previously exotic elements, flows along with characteristic forthrightness and with the charm of sophistication mixed with abounding goodwill.

Even in his written language, fluent as it is, Moorty retains a slight tang of his background. And in this flavored language, he teaches us all how it is possible to be different from each other and yet to reach out confident of human response whenever the riches of individuality are permitted free play in the art of a generous scholar and a rare spirit.

-William Stafford
Library of Congress Poet
United States Poet Laureate 1970

Why Was She Forced to Lose Her Long, Flowing, Dark Hair?

I

It was more than sixty years ago
In a remote Brahmin hamlet
Of about thirteen cheerful households,
Nestled amidst coconut and mango groves,
Kissed by the stale green waters of the nearby pond,
Not too far from the sacred Godavary River.

Her house at the edge of the village
Seemed robust and wholesome,
Guarded by the friendly breeze of cheerful neighbors.

On one sultry summer morning,
Loud cries blasted my tender drowsy ears;
Waves of bursts of deafening cries shattered the still houses.
I streamed out of my grandfather's ancient house

And rushed toward the source of those unending cries;
Other neighbors had already pooled there.

II

The young woman's lord had died.
That fair woman in crumpled red saree
With long, dark, curly hair cried and cried.
I thought she would finally remain still
Like her husband's cold still body;

Now she smashed her jingling glass bangles
That adorned her still wrists;
She wiped the red dot from her fair forehead.

III

And on that fateful tenth day,
A merciless village barber
Would shave her dark, long, flowing hair.
And it was the long-held tradition,
She would unwillingly perpetuate:
Sans joy, sans bliss, sans sex, sans fate,
Only to exist, to dream, and to mourn.
I then vaguely learnt the cruelty
Of traditions that hold no promise of hope.

A Prayer Addressed to Lord of Death

O Yama, God of Death, wield not your arrogant power!
Shield me from your wrath and dark terror.
You well know that you'll triumph.

Why then would you rush like a scared deer toward
My precious life? Let me demand of you sacred pact:
Grant me fearlessness; allow me to yield not soon to your
power.

On First Watching Attenborough's 'Gandhi'

When only a buoyant twelve-year-old boy,
Visiting my grandfather in Kothiviri Agraharam,
A remote Brahmin village, near the confluence
Of the sacred Godavary River's waters and the Bay of Bengal.
I heard on that late January evening the deafening news
Of Gandhi's assassination in a faraway place.

Suddenly the cold evening of New Delhi
Dispatched a frightening shiver to my warm village!
For many days my playful activities had no momentum.
There was no breeze; the tall coconut and palm trees
Stood motionless in deference to the Great Soul's departure.
Perhaps the river too ceased to flow.

My confused emotions became frozen and fossilized.
Thirty-five years after, Attenborough's "Gandhi" thawed
them.
Now my adult thoughts connect India, England, and America

Monkey Army at Tirumalai Hills, South India – The Abode of Lord Venkateswara

They are all over Tirumalai Hills.
They assault you with their surprise attacks!
Surely, they are as crafty as we are.

They leap, jump, swing from banyan branches!
They dart across passing cars!
They maul the unwary pilgrims!
They pounce on the innocent children!

I wonder at the deference the humans
Demonstrate toward the descendants
Of the famed monkey-god, Hanuman,
The loyal lieutenant of Lord Rama!

On First Looking at the Lord of the Seven Hills

I beheld the deep noon sky
Bowing down to touch the last
Manmade steps as I climbed up
The top of the sacred hill.

My dear father and I, a seven-year-old,
After several tiring hours and hundreds of steep steps
From Chandragiri to the summit of Tirupati,
Saw the glorious shining top of the temple.

My father then bent to whisper that
The beckoning temple was the eternal abode
Of the Father of all fathers—
Lord Venkateswara of the Tirumalai Hills.

Struck by the magic spell of the distant
Symphony of holy sounds and mantras,
I obeyed my father's commands
And finally completed my sacred journey.

After a long and tired wait, I felt, saw, and heard
The dark idol of Venkateswara's solid
Image shine like gold foil flutter in wind.
The priests in unison muttered verses sacred.

I couldn't pray; confused I was!
The radiance of the Lord's holiness
Elevated me to new heights.

Seventy years later and ten thousand miles away,
He is the same to me as He was then!

Karma I

Still fenced by the barbed wire
Of the sinful deeds of his past life,
Now monotonously mumbles
Words of His holy name,
Stretches his skinny, wrinkled, wretched
Hands toward the rushing indifferent pilgrims.

His body, a mere withered branch,
Leans against the trembling beanpole!

Karma II

The leprosy-stricken beggar in tattered clothes,
Leaning against his shaky bean pole,
Extending his brown grimy empty bowl,
Stands near the temple entrance;
Envies those garishly attired pilgrims
Dashing for holy sight of God's image,
Waits for sacred mercy to be showered on him.
Blames his fate for his present wretched plight.

Crossing Godavary River by Train in Third-Class Compartment

The wobbly speeding train obeyed commands
Of the aged fragile bridge, subduing
The huddled passengers of the compartment
Crane their necks, brush their sweltering faces,
Jostle their sticky brown bodies,
To behold below the almost motionless
Blue and brown waters of the Godavery, to throw
Copper coins carrying the weight
Of the poor souls' unheard prayers.

The river's distant holiness seemed
Indifferent to the profanity of stench—
Of poverty, of sweat, of unwashed latrines, of dried vomit.

As a seven-year-old boy, then, I bore all filth and suffering.
Now, as an adult, I question man's capacity to bear such.

Notes: Godavary River flows mostly through the state of Andhra Pradesh, South India.

Walking by Godavary River on a Rainy Evening

When I was a boy of five,
My mother once whispered that the
River Godavary was a Great Mother.
And the gentle sounds of its waters echoed
In my ears for several flowing years,
Farther though the river was.

When I was in seventh grade,
My geography books portrayed
The river's origins at Nasik Triyumbuk
In the west, its limping flow eastward,
Gently cutting narrow gorges of eastern
Ghats, the hilly ranges, affectionately
Joining the Bay of Bengal.

When I was a teenager, once I walked
By the hallowed river on a rainy evening.
That was the first time ever I looked
At the river closely. Then I felt the beat
Of the river's roar drowning my mother's
Sacred whispers of long past years.

The river seemed gorgeous in its turbulence;
Its raw, rushing waters were ferocious
Like demons of Vedas; the tiny scattered
Dinghies floated like prancing horses.

I mused. Befuddled between myth and naked
Reality, I couldn't reconcile that Lord Rama
And his beloved Sita of Ramayana had
Their sacred abode on the river's banks.

I mused. Befuddled between myth and naked
Reality, I couldn't reconcile that Lord Rama
And his beloved Sita of Ramayana had
Their sacred abode on the river's banks.

Notes: Lord Rama and his devoted wife, Sita, are the hero and
heroine of the Hindu epic 'Ramayana'.

Godavary River in Floods

The silent motionless flow
With angry burst of monsoons
Galloped and crashed against the gentle banks.

The lean and hungry cows shivered in fright;
The fishermen's brown boats fought
For life like chickens without heads.

The pale blue waters lost their luster;
The lifeless logs by the brown muddy banks
Gained a new life and energy of force
As they hurried down ferociously.

Now the holiness of the river
Disappeared; some devilish form
Assumed its rule and spread martial law.

When the terror of the horror
Loses its force, my Godavary
Will regain her natural gentle flow
And reinforce my perpetual faith.

After all, Godavary's rage
Can't reign eternally.

What do the mere earthlings do
When mighty gods are ferocious?
Oh! We simply pray!

Godavary River in Summer

Your sacredness shriveled up like a putrefied mango!
Your vast holiness reduced to a paltry sum of water!
Your swelling bosom mishandled, metamorphosed into
Heaps of dusty sand dunes stretching into horizon!

Who was the merciless rapist? Who was the culprit?

Did the tropical sun steal your waters in broad daylight?
Did the scorching fellow suck you to quench his thirst?
Did the bloodsucker strip you to reveal your unholy plight?

What do I behold? Your ageless sanctity mingled in stench!

Immutability

Far beyond the solemn waters
Of the sleepy Godavary River,
The ancient sun rises slowly
To chase away the lingering darkness.

Here on the steep banks
Enveloped by the brown moist earth,
The calm steel-gray waters,
The deep blue sky recently brightened by the hurrying sun,
A lone crow on the edge of a banyan branch,
Now beaten by sharp beams,
Flutters and shoots into infinite space.

Just at that moment,
I open my eyes from confusing meditation.
At that instant,
I realize the immutability of the sun and the sky
And the seasonal changes of Godavary.

Here and There

My bare feet sink into the clammy sand
As I watch a tiny open boat drift toward
The rushing deep waters of the flooded
Godavery carrying the burden of life's misery.

There in the midst of troubled waters,
Father and son share their bonds,
Spread their net, struggle to catch the gliding fish.

Here, on the banks, beaten by the sharp sun,
I suffer the turbulence of the dead fish stench.

Meditation at Godavary

All the black and brown bodies that shimmered
And the shrunken faces that revealed embittered
Tales of fury and misery were a community that shared
A common boat of life with dead fish and
Huddled crying frightened children.

Now the individual passengers trickled
Out of the boat bare-footed onto the hot, glowing
Sands of life. Some women carried basked loads
Of fish; others suspended gazing children on their shoulders.

While I stood under the banyan tree's shade,
Staring at the streaming human parade,
My eyes gathered the river's vastness pitted
Against 'the still sad music of humanity'
That drowned in the roar of the mighty river.

The river will embrace the wide lap of Bay of Bengal;
Those men, women, and children will move on
With their journey toward their karmic destinations.

My meditation on life and soul, peace and love,
Under the shade of the giant tree is now disturbed
And overshadowed by the sad spectacle I beheld

The Path Yet to Be Made

Still the hilltop fills in me
A pleasure immeasurable.
Beyond the dusty village boundaries,
The little round mound stands
Like an ancient sentinel in ruins.

The winding crooked path from my house
May take me years to reach the summit.
My villager's dark stories of
Ghosts and spirits have kept me
Home dull, long, and lonely.

In future, I may still venture out
And step by step painfully ascend;
Perhaps avoid the beaten path, and
Yet hope to chart a new one.

Anyway, I am tired of the old folklore:
Let me start afresh one for future winds!
Who knows, the gentle winds may yet
Gradually flatten the haunted mound
By blowing away the dirt around it and
Leaving no scars of the dim past for glory to come!

On Looking at Banyan Tree

I

You—the giant canopy of God, rooted firmly
In the brown bowels of the earth,
Spreading your sturdy arms to shelter
The sweltering tired farmers returning
From planting green paddy saplings—stagger me.
To you, I bow!

II

We, the truant boys, baked in mud after
A senseless bath in the green stagnant waters
Of the nearby pool, find you a welcome retreat;
The monkeys with their chirping babes on their back
Seek refuge in the laps of your branches.
We, like monkeys, swing from one aerial root to another
Yet, you bear us ungrudgingly.
We worship you for your forbearance!

III

You are the sentinel of our village.
All the drooping elders gather under your expensive
Shade for their deliberations and chatter.
You are our natural open community center.
We are grateful to you!

IV

You're the nourisher of our village poet's muse;
You bless any philosopher's musings.
Are you your great, great, great grandfather
That inspired Siddhartha to attain the Buddhahood
And led millions of disciples spread his gospel
Like your aerial roots that further convert into Multitudes
Of trunks?
You are the king among trees.

V

You are not like mango tree
Or banana tree
Or coconut tree;
These we find in our grandfathers' backyards.
Your permanence and royalty baffle me.

VI

You are a protector, a nourisher, a provider
Of life and shelter without bearing fruit!
You stand firm to support our play and intrigues.
And all that helps us is sacred!

VII

To you, I sing; to you, I bow!
You are a challenge to man!
You were here yesterday!
You are here today!
Your children will be here tomorrow!

Song of Hope

Koil perches on banyan bough
With its refrain of koohoo, koohoo;
Pierces the sweltering stillness
Of the tropical summer afternoon.

Between its notes, I hear my
Heartbeat thump, thump.

The notes, the shade, and my heartbeat
Drive away the steady merciless sun.

Hope is koil's song;
Hope is banyan's shade;
Hope is the music of the self.

Notes: 'Koil' is a common Indian bird; perhaps koil is similar
to nightingale

My House of Hope

I made my hope a house
Built with red bricks of kindness;
Roofed with beams of love;
Carpeted with pastels of affection;
Draped with fabrics of empathy.
But fools stubbornly refuse
To behold my simple cornucopian affluence.

Lines Composed upon Reading a Line – "God, Ever-Present Divine Principle Is Always with Us."

No room for my temple in my small town!
I'm far removed to visit His abode.
And I've lived here for over three decades.

Yet, in my house of brick and mortar,
Daily I bow before my God—a mere
Picture on decrepit paper and just an
Image carved in bronze and shining,
A simple artifact housed in my kitchen cupboard—
Utter ancient mystical syllables
And offer silently my prayers.

My ninety-six-year-old father, who
Lived far away and beyond the oceans
And passed away a decade ago, tended
Me spiritually with his blessings.

My God! He hasn't bestowed on me riches;
Yet His immanence nourishes my being
To face the world compressed by
Terror, fear, hatred, and prejudice.

My Grandfather Died in the Holy City

Several years after
His reported death,
His image of a living
Grandfather stood before me.

A pious man he was.
I could only travel back
To two summers of my childhood.
He found in me a fond grandson.

Suddenly, one summer came
The news—apocryphal it was
I thought; he wouldn't return
To our village anymore.

It was rumored that he died
In Ganga's holy waters at Kaasi!
Did he drown by the ghat?
Or, was he swallowed by the cold currents?

No one knew how he died;
Or, when he died.
We in the village knew he lived a holy life
And died in a sacred and revered river.

II

After several decades, now, once in a while,
My rusty frozen tears thaw
Upon my thoughts of him
And gently trickle down my hardened cheeks,
The same that once were softly squeezed
By my beloved grandfather.

III

After several decades, now, once in a while,
My rusty frozen tears thaw
Upon my thoughts of him
And gently trickle down my hardened cheeks,
The same that once were softly squeezed
By my beloved grandfather.
I realize now memories don't fade away
Like drifting summer clouds.

Notes: 'Ganga' is known usually as 'Kaasi' or Benares, or
Varanasi.
'Ghat' is a stone slab leading to the edge of a river's waters.

God vs. Man

Will that stony God ever smile,
Shower blessings upon the crowded
Silent jaded pilgrims
That reach the remote top of
The sacred seven hills, disgorged
Tortuously by exhausted buses?

Either the immense, rich, dark God
Is immeasurably wealthy, beyond
Petty human calculations, or, those
Emptied devotees share a common
Blind trust in that idol that stands
Shielded by all the solid gold and
Liquid money that is loaded every
Minute in that ever-swelling 'hundi'.

After a lapse of twelve long years,
I too became for a few hours
A part of that exhausted humanity.

Notes: 'The sacred seven hills' refers to Tirumalai Hills
(Tirupati) in Andhra Pradesh State of South India.

'Hundi' denotes a large canvas receptacle that is placed close
to the Lord Venkateswara's idol in the temple; the devotees
dropping jewelry and cash into it to signify fulfillment of their
vows.

Soul!

I don't notice it; I've heard about it.
I know I've a mind encased in my brain.
I realize I've a heart 'cause it beats.

What about soul, my atma!

How do I notice it?
How do I realize it?
Is it the spirit of man?
If so, where is it hidden?
I can't show it, nor can you!

May be, soul is like God, the Brahman!
May be, soul is like air!
May be, soul is like headache.

It's there! We can't see it!
It continues to tease us!
It's a mystery that we all like.

What's There in Name?

My spirit though nameless is spirit still;
It is ever-present and recognized by all.
It is there.

Hinduism, Judaism, Buddhism, Taoism,
Confucianism, Christianity, Islam, Calvinism,
Jainism, Zoroastrianism, Sikhism, Mormonism—
Are known all over the world.
Yes, all these relate to my spirit.

But my spirit has no name.
Still it is known as Spirit—
One without physical attributes.

Ganges, Yangtze, Mississippi, Amazon,
Congo, Thames, Danube, Don, Volga
Are the rivers we all know.
They all carry water; their flow is eternal.
But water has no name.
Yet it is called water.

Oh! What's there in name!
God and spirit are unnamable.
But they're omnipresent and immutable
Like the sun and the moon—
God and Spirit will continue to be beyond us!

Love and Fear

In the late fifties when I visited Taj Mahal,
Where love is entombed,
Love sprouted in me.

In the late sixties when I viewed Mahatma Gandhi's Samadhi,
Where nonviolence is interred,
Hatred in me vanished, joining the atmosphere.

In the mid-eighties when I neared Check Point Charley,
Where love and hatred, violence, and nonviolence
Are trapped and undermined,
On a cold and gloomy April afternoon,
A fear unknown enveloped me.

Notes: Samadhi: the hallowed ground where a body is cremated with an enclosed wall surrounding it.

New Delhi Summer

As I stepped out of the Air India Boeing
On a steamy June early morning,
The still-trapped heat scorched my cool body;
Sweat began to soak my clothes freely;
The radiant heat's cacophony benumbed me.

II

My memory of the distant Jamuna River seemed
A mirage of mere brown sluggish stream;
Perhaps even the river waters evaporated
To quench the parched dry sun.

III

The taxi ride on the dusty, dry roads lined
With hungry trees, choked and exhausted trucks,
Lazy bullock carts pulled by thirsty bulls
Dragged on and on forever.

IV

The merciless sun drenched the white heat.
The afternoon dust storm blanketed the vacant sky
With golden dust particles blinding the driver
To swerve toward invisible lanes loaded with scooters
And automobiles making me shiver with fright with no AC
on.

V

In the past, for several years I bore the brunt of stultifying heat
Of New Delhi summers with no complaint.
Now, after a seven-year absence, I couldn't bear it.
I realize then being used to pain from the beginning
And then experiencing comfort is different from moving
From to comfort and pleasure to pain and suffering.

Disunity in Unity

I crave for what my eye sees,
But my eye sees not within me.
Oedipus and Gloucester saw truth
Only with their inward eye.
What appears real is illusion.
What is real is invisible.

Oh! I am caught in the net of desires.
My eye is like a fisherman that is
Eager to trap me; my sight baits
My mind. Why? Why? Why?

What a beauty is insight!
Is not sight a gift of God?
How noble in its inner power!
Is not truth then my sight of God?

Self-Sufficiency or Self-Reliance!

How exhausted am I trying to be self-sufficient!
How expensive it is to buy a snapper for my lawn
That I mow grudgingly only a few times in the long, hot
Summers.
How unwise is it to own a pickup truck and a chainsaw
To cut and haul wood for warmth in winter!

I've noticed my neighbors grease their hands on weekends
And monotonously fetch wood from the nearby mountains.
But they don't observe me pursue my engaging reading.
They don't seem to fathom my spiritual self-reliance.
How cruel of them to label me 'weird'!

If some curious one were to ask me unmindfully—
"Which do you prefer: self-sufficiency or self-reliance?"—
After all, who will do my reading of Emerson and Thoreau?
Mowing lawn and fetching wood can be handled by others!

In Meditation

I cogitate, sit cross-legged, and meditate
Glorifying gods as my invisible friends and recite
Mystical verses silently seeking their blessings 'cause
I don't see them. But it is their immanence,
Their pervasive spirit that provides solace
To my troubled spirit and offers guidance.
And I don't need a temple or a church or a congregation
To think about God and to offer prayers to him.

I perform my meditation daily religiously
Yet I need the names of gods to relate to them.
The ancient Greeks invoked their Apollo and Zeus;
Today's Hindus still invoke Brahma, Vishnu, Maheshwara,
Rama, Krishna, and Shirdi and Satya Saibaba.
So, I recite ancient verses in solitude for solace.

Notes: Brahma, Vishnu, Maheshwara: The Hindu holy trinity
representing Creation, Preservation, and Dissolution, yet
representing the three phases of one God

Rama and Krishna: The incarnations of Lord Vishnu that
appear in the two Hindi epics 'Ramayama' and
'Mahabharata'

Shirdi and Satya Baba: 20th-century spiritual figures
endowed with mystical Powers who preached love and
forgiveness are revered by their worshippers around the
world.

Who Am I?

I am brown;
I am different
From the white and the black.
I am Dravidian, a word as
Mysterious as the origin
Of the universe.
Now I am hyphenated American;
I speak English
With a discernible accent,
But my students loved it.
It's not Southern Utah accent;
It's not South Indian Brahmin accent, either.
Oh! South Indian accent
Is perhaps rooted in Telugu,
Tamil, Kannada, or Malayalam.
Or, is it a composite one,
The composite one that is
Further nurtured by your
School, teachers, and peers?
While I was growing up in south India,
I was still a minority:
Because I was a Brahmin;
Because I was not rich like Rreddys or Kammas.
While I was in New Delhi,
I was still a minority.
I sharply felt it so then.

First, my name gave out;
Second, my Hindi was tinged
With a distinct South-Indian accent;

Third, I was a shade darker than the fair Punjabi;
Fourth, I was brighter than the others
In my mixed Indian circle;
Fifth, I was able to speak their tongue,
While they couldn't my language;
It was exotic and foreign to them;
Sixth, for that matter,
They couldn't even pronounce
My mouthful Godly name;
Seventh, I was cultured and
Knew Gita and Shakespeare,
Saw popular Bombay movies

And attended Krishnamurti's
Discourses on metaphysics and theology;
Missed no major classical concerts
Or dance performances—eastern or western.
Yet, I was different for being poor.

I am what I am.
Why should I be like someone else?
Even my brothers are different.
We share the same parents.

I am brown
I am different
From the white and the black.
The Upanishads say
"Tat Tvum asi."
"That thou art."

Notes

Dravidian: of South India different from North
India, considered the original
natives of India

Brahmin: The highest caste in the hierarchy
of the traditional Hindu caste
system

South India: Essentially of Dravidian culture
with four major languages—
Telugu, Tamil, Kannada, and
Mayalam—each with its own
script and linguistic origins

Hindi: The national language of the
independent India, also one of the
major languages of North India

Punjabi: of North India in the state of Punjab

Gita: Short form for Bhagavad Gita
(Song of the Blessed Lord), the
great devotional classic of
Hinduism, renowned as the jewel
of India's spiritual wisdom and
represents the essence of
Hinduism, much as the Sermon on
the Mount presents the essence of
Christianity

J. Krishnamurti: Considered one of the greatest
                    thinkers of our age who influenced
                    millions throughout the twentieth
                    century

Upanishads: a series of mystical and philosophic
                    prose works in a dialog form
                    constituting the chief theological
                    documents of ancient Hinduism—
                    a total of 108 discourses that can be
                    dated to about 600 BC.

Kammas   and   Reputed to be affluent members of
Reddys: agricultural community of Andhra

Tat Tvum Asi: translated from Sanskrit language,
                    the ancient classical language of
                    India, similar to Latin, means "That
                    thou art." Taken from Chandogya
                    Upanishad, this famous

Expression identifies the relationship between the
individual and the Absolute.

Passage from India
(Inspired by Walt Whitman's 'Passage to India')

I

You, the hallowed land of ancient myths and mighty religions,
Of Hindus, Muslims, Christians,
Of Buddhists, Jains, Parsees, and Sikhs;
Of multiple languages, of diverse cultures;
Of Buddha, Ashoka, and Mahatma Gandhi;
Of temples, mosques, churches, and gurdwaras;
Of sacred rivers—Ganga, Jamuna, Godavary, and Kaveri—
Of Konarak and Khajuraho; of Ajanta and Ellora;
Of Qutub Minar and Taj Mahal;
Gave me life and fed me virtues and values.

II

Your tender heart for art, sculpture, and dance;
Your variegated mind for truth and science;
Your noble spirit for tolerance
Baffle me and elevate me.

III

Your mystical fusion of past, present, and yet to come
Confuse me.
Columbus set his sails in pursuit of your spicy shores;
Emerson, Thoreau, and Whitman gravitated toward your

Holy, mysterious, and mystical spirit.

IV

Your sacred spirit still haunts me in the
Lap of my adopted mother, America.
Though firm and secure in the bosom of my new mother,

V

Your sacred spirit still haunts me in the
Lap of my adopted mother, America.
Though firm and secure in the bosom of my new mother,
Nourished by the sturdy arms of the Rockies,
I still cherish you, India. And I admire you America—
The two sisters of the same Mother!

VI

Now, my two children of their natural mother, America,
Drawn to the aura of their father's motherland,
Are eager to touch the shores of their grandmother.

VII

O! America and India,
I sing joyously to the glory of both.
You two sisters are apart only
In distance and time!
But your spirits sing in unison,
Undaunted by the discordant elements.

VIII

Om, Santhi! Om, santhi!! Om, santhihi!!!

Notes

Buddhists and Jains: followers of Buddhism and Jainism, the two religions that emerged out of Hinduism during 5th century BCE

Parsees: followers of Zoroastrian religious sect in India—the practitioners of which were driven out of Persia by the Muslims in the eighth century AD

Sikhs: followers of Sikhism that emerged out of Hinduism in 15th century AD

Ashoka: Emperor Ashoka belongs to the first great Indian empire which came to power in 312 BCE. He was committed to peace and goodwill through spread of Buddhism.

Gurdwara: It is the place of worship for Sikhs.

Konarak: The Great Sun Temple was built in the 13th century by a Hindu king in Orissa State.

Khajuraho: has the largest group of medieval Hindu and Jain temples, famous for their erotic sculptures in the State of Madhya Pradesh, founded in the 15th century

Ajanta: The Buddhist caves of Ajanta date from 200 BCE to 650 AD. World Heritage site in the state of Maharashtra

Ellora: Cave temples of rock-cut architecture representing Hindu, Buddhist, and Jain faiths in the State of Maharashtra, a World Heritage site

Qutub Minar: a soaring minaret (tower) of victory of the onset of Muslim rule in India, near New Delhi; it is the tallest tower in India, a landmark.

Taj Mahal: the world-renowned extravagant monument in white marble for love built by Emperor Shah Jahan as a monument for his second wife, Mumtaz Mahal, who died in childbirth in 1631. It was started in 1631 and completed in 1653.

Om: sacred invocation representing the absolute essence of the divine principle

Shanthi: "Peace that passeth understanding." (T.S. Eliot)

A Hymn to Agni

You, the Vedic priest of sacrifices!
You, the nourisher, purifier, and destroyer!
You, the conveyor of human wishes to gods!
You, the presiding flame at Hindu weddings and cremations!
You, the kindling spark of my imagination!
Ignite me with poetic creation and release my fear.

Lord Rama of Ramayana invoked your guidance to test
His beloved Sita's purity after her rescue from the evil
Ravana.
In all your flaming glory, you proved to Rama, Sita's virtue.

I now burn with desire to know the real you.
Are you a Vedic God or a primeval priest of yore.
Or, are you just a wildfire out to destroy that is irrelevant?

I can handle you in small doses, but don't engulf me.
To you, I pray. Grant me fire of imagination and creativity.

My Mother, Annapoornamma!

I

When I came across the title of a journal 'Annapoorna',
Memories of my late 'amma' whose name 'Annapoorna'
Flooded my aged mind; she proudly justified her existence
To the core as a human incarnation of the goddess.

II

During 'rationing' time in the 1940s in India,
My handicapped mother would cook rice
In earthen pots and serve it mixed with lentil soup,
Eggplant curry, tender banana plant trunk chutney
In a big stainless steel bowl and place small balls in our
cupped palms—
Four young brothers seated around—to make sure we were all
Fed equitably the meager food, leaving very little unto herself.

III

What a noble soul she was!
At the ritualistic conclusion of each meal,
We would all chant in unison "Anna data sukhi bhava,"—
May the donor of food be blessed with happiness.

IV

Surely, so she is now in heaven happy having lived
Her existence cooking and feeding her hungry children.
The taste of her deliciously cooked and lovingly served
Food still lingers in my mouth even after sixty-five years.

A Hamlet of Brahmin Widows

As a boy of eleven, I noticed
Several head-shaven Brahmin widows
Clad in plain white sarees and heads
Scantily covered, devoid of bras and blouses,
Whose lives were confined to their kitchens.
I never realized then how widowhood
Had erased their lives in my grandfather's
Brahmin hamlet wafted only by the stale breeze
Of the stagnant green pond that we boys
Used as a swimming pool nestled amidst coconut
And mango groves and green paddy fields!

The widows continued to be the passengers
Of my memory; though the sharpness of my
Memory has faded, their phantoms still haunt me.
May be it was their karma; the present is different.

Sitting at Home on a Sunday Morning While My Neighbors Go to Church

Still clad in pyjamas, I silently offer my prayers
To the copper and bronze idols in my kitchen
Cupboard; while my neighbors decked in Sunday
Dress motor down to their church, just two blocks away.
I recite in solitude ancient Sansktrit verses and yet look up
At the clear blue sky and keep sipping my steaming coffee.
I don't feel forced to go to temple even if we had one.
The sacred place of my worship is my kitchen.

How I pray and when I should pray is my own choice.
Surely, I think of the Divine daily, quietly like my
Heartbeat unseen but felt. I enjoy my coffee as I pray.
Simply, I listen to my inner self!

Driving in Blinding Snowstorm

I glued my glazed eyes to the fogged-up windshield;
The galloping battalions of snowflakes strained my eyes;
The marginal road merged mercilessly into the endless night
That refused to open up to my assaulted sight.

The white slick road meandered,
While the gentle pounding of flakes cursed my plight.

The ugliness of the unexpected April storm
Couldn't match the heavenly Christmas snow.

Being on the road on a snowy night is different
From being at home by warm fireplace.

Snow in Spring!!!

Where are you spring? Here! No!
You seem to be still lingeringly drowsy!
Yesterday I thought you were wide-awake!
May be, it was a teasing transitory break!

Today, you're back to your usual fickle
Self, playing hide and seek with us mortals.
How can we trust nature that is indifferent?
We were all mentally and physically ready—

For spring that has yet to make up its mood.
Mother Nature—We don't trust you anymore.
Yet, I trust in God 'cause He is invisible.

The trees around us that were gleeful yesterday
Are now wilted and sadly bearing your evil burden!
Winter! You need to hibernate now! Don't tease us!

Lift-Off Toward Heavens

Lips pursed,
Hands clasped,
Stomachs wrenched,
Hearts pounded.
Chills blazed through our backs—
"Three, two, one"
"Lift off... The Discovery"—
A collective sigh of relief!

The grey clouds of doubts
Were dispersed by the white smoke of Discovery
Like autumnal leaves swept by fierce winds.
Now, the Discovery pierced the blue sky.

It was a challenge, America,
To rediscover ourselves and to
Revitalize our strength and hope.

The Dark Anniversary

I

Anniversaries like nature's seasons come and go,
And fade slowly, wither in course of time like
Drooping drying brittle roses in green vase on redbrick
mantel,
But the global anniversary lodged in our collective memory,
Entombed in the waking world's mangled consciousness,
Twisted by bloodthirsty satanic minions,
Still haunts us of its colossal heinousness.
It is an anniversary unlike any in human history.
It's a day that has become a part of us all.
It's a day mournfully us of infernal callousness
Inflicted on humanity and indelibly scorched in world history.

II

My heart-wrenching visit to the Holocaust
Museum in Washington, D.C. agonizingly sharpened my
sight
On the power of intolerance of insane religious zealots with
no sight.

III

The twin World Trade Center's towers that piously and loftily
housed
All religions, all cultures—the beacon of hope for the entire
world—

Were abruptly scorched by twin jets misguided by soulless, demonic
Terrorists in their unholy mission desecrating the sacred soil of hope,
Democracy, faith, and human dignity.

IV

Suddenly on that fateful day, the world was made unsafe for humanity;
Is there a reason for God's creation of such inhuman humans
Imprisoned in their bigotry reducing humans to ashes?

V

My god! Terrorism, evil man's creation is cowardice;
Terrorism that has since plagued the world is soulless.
Terrorism is the first refuge of the religious scoundrel
Who has no faith in self and in others.
It is born out of colossal ignorance and massive stupidity.
Terrorism is unholy and a blight on humanity.
It is a deadly poisonous snake sneakily lurking behind bushes!

VI

Eighteen years ago, we all witnessed a painful, corrosive change—
A change that altered forever our assumptions and hopes.
From that day we've marched ahead slowly, mindful,
With a sacred oath, with a collective determination, with a radically altered consciousness.
We vowed never to have that kind of day again,
Never, never again!

VII

Life, liberty, pursuit of happiness—
The inherent rights of humans around the world—
Ought not to be a hostage of insane religious bigots.
That 21st century's Holocaust of September 11, 2001
Remains forever a burden on the humanity.
It's not America's burden alone—the land
Of all religions, all tongues, all cultures—;
It's not just one nation's agony!
It's the world's burden!
It's all nations' shared and cumulative agony and grief!

VIII

Let us all then bear the burden.
The World Trade Center brought the global economy
together.
Let us then bear our sacred mutual responsibilities.
Let us remember never to forget what happened on that fateful
day
Eighteen years ago.
Let us toll a death knell to terrorism!
Let us ring in a world free from shackles of religious bigotry,
Devoid of cowardice and fear;
Let us resolve to forge ahead and fight terrorism.

IX

The future generations will visit Ground Zero Museum
And recognize the pain, suffering, and human loss
Inflicted by the filthy hands and corroded minds of terrorists
And chant "Never, Never again."
"We'll not let history repeat itself."
The eternal flames of trust and faith in humanity will burn
forever

A Quick Visit to the Temple of Poseidon by a Luxury Tourist Bus

Those stately mute pillars of the temple of Poseidon
Stood erect, unruffled by the ageless gentle wind.
Straight down below and far into the merging horizon.
The deceptive still waters of the Aegean Sea silently gaze
At the deep blue sky spread like a giant spokeless umbrella.

The Japanese, the American, and the sundry excited
Tourists clicked their Nikons in Chorus—
To freeze the remnants of the past arrogantly for the vague
posterity
While the amorphous history's vastness girdled, the tired
Tourists quickly retreated into shifting shade and guzzled the
Athenian beer.

Sunset in Mykanos, the Greek Island

Spread against the calm Aegean blue waters
On the light greenish horizon
There hung a giant grapefruit!
Ah! That is nature in its pure glory!

My beholding the sunset from hilltop
Imparted a new dimension to the never ending Nature
When all my perturbed ecological concerns dissipated
Like the fast diminishing sunset that was ready
To swallow the orange disk into the waiting waters.

Ah! As the world spreads it skirt, my faith in
Nature is renewed though man has repeatedly manhandled it.

Sunset in Santorini, Greek Island

Sitting in the roof garden of Café del Mor e Sol,
Perched on the jagged cliffs of Santorini,
Sipping Mythos beer, listening to Mozart and Vivaldi,
Watching the sun's grapefruit-size orange disc,
Sinking slowly into the Aegean waters and the horizon—
Is a sight and ambience that I'll remember for ever
Since it soothes my troubled spirits, makes me oblivious
To the terror-stricken world that surrounds me.

The sunset was uplifting, memorable, and dazzling.
All the tourists' eyes, who assembled for the sight,
Were riveted toward the sinking sun, leaving behind
A slice of it for a moment for us all to remember.

The big world is around us and with us all the time;
The nature that is amidst us will always be our solace!

The Old Mop Lady of Building Number Three, Moldova State University

The drooping aged Moldovan woman
Draped in long, tight, dark-blue apron,
Hooded in pastel floral scarf,
Dips the long mop into an aluminum pail,
Pulls it out, bends down, moves it up and down,
Back and forth on the well-trodden hard floor.

She repeats the chore several times through the day.
It is the same pail of dirty water.
The mop too is pitiably grimy.
Surely she must have aged performing the routine for years.

Meanwhile, the rushing, bouncing careless students
Come and go unmindful of the mopped floor,
Wet and smelly without glow.

As I watch her while I sip my coffee,
I realize that she too earns her daily bread
By the sweat of her tired arms and hunched back!
She too has a life to live!

Yet she at work is a sight to behold!
I still see the past at work in the present!
After all, old routines linger on
And the old order of the Soviets hasn't faded yet!
Ah! Surely, old habits die hard!

Notes: Here, the 'past' refers to the fact that Moldova was in the past a part of the Soviet Union; now, it is an independent country.

"Hi Noroc!"

John Keats' ecstasy on beholding Grecian Urn
Prompted him declare, "Beauty is Truth!"
The young poet's reading Chapman's Homer
Spiraled him to behold the sky and watch stars swimming.

On one cold, wintry, snow-filled Chisinau evening,
My Moldovan cohorts assembled around me,
Initiated me into their sacredly coveted ritual,
By offering me Moldovan fabricated Vodka
In tiny, foggy, gilt-edged chalises, half-filled.

My initial nervous hesitation evaporated
As I imbibed the white clear potent liquid slowly and
expectantly.

Coaxed further, I soon became a part of the tradition.
Now they all chanted as in a choir, "Hi Noroc, Hi Noroc!"
I then muttered gazing at the chandelier, "Spirits are
pleasurable!"

Notes: 'Noroc' is the Moldovan expression equivalent to
'cheers'.

Martishor to You, Moldova!

Moldova marches majestically,
On to a new path strewn with smiles;
Laced with vibrant youth meandering dutifully,
Dusted by nascent democratic spirits,
On to its dynamic 'self' as a 'nation';
Versed in carefully chartered destiny,
Adumbrated now by a cheerful generation.

Notes: 'Martishor' is the official celebration of the first day
of spring on 1st March throughout Moldova.

The Cats of Sanaa, Yemen

Those lean and feeble cats
Dart under fleeting *Toyotas*.
Leap into the fly-swarmed trash bins
That contain several days'
Garbage in pregnant plastic sacks—
Of tiny empty milk cartons
Of rotten eggs in smithereens,
Of soggy lettuce heads,
Of cigarette butts,
Of mutilated meat pieces,
Of wiry dry chicken breasts—
Piled high
To scavenge and salvage.

Maybe they find some edible food!
Why would strain
Tricks of leaping into and tossing out
All that is discarded?

Their new-found treats are an
Offspring of hunger;
Their sad *meaows* are dull, long, shrill
Like sick babies' cries;
They have neither patrons nor masters!
These orphans simply fend for themselves—
Darting out of rugged narrow streets,
Jumping out of dusty brown trees, mud walls,
Cleverly escaping from under
Menacing dababs' jumping wheels, erring automobiles—
Uncertain of their future.

I have heard more cats' shrieks
In Sanaa than at any other place.
My path is strewn with an assortment of cats!
They too want to live and find a place!

Notes: 'Dababs' are covered three-wheeled motorcycles used
as taxis in Sanaa.

Lines Conceived upon an Adventurous Maiden Marathon 'Qat'-Chewing Session

We stepped into the inviting room—
Snoozing alongside three walls, bright blue,
Sunsetred, corn-yellow, coffee-brown elbow
Cushions in the embrace of silken soft floor seats.

Our cheerful host picked up
Each of the pink, blue, and white plastic-wrapped,
Yet unsqueezed 'qat' bouquets that seemed
Like raw pearls in oyster shells, and tossed them
At each of us—sharply aimed!

The room's variegated colors dazzled us,
While the airborne 'qat' bouquets landed in our laps.

Our energetic and beaming host left us
For more mysterious embellishments.

Soon, he materialized holding Hadda mineral
Water bottles that seemed like baptismal water.
As the western sun blessed us, we squatted
Like maharajahs in their private chambers.

Our kind host left us, onvoking 'In sha Allah',
This will be a sacred initiation!

Upon his return, he placed in front of us
Tall thermoses loaded with Qishr, partially opened

Canada Dry soft drinks, two empty glasses,
Perfumed facial tissue boxes, hot pink ashtrays.
A tall jar of huddled ice cubes stood in the center.

Now the tender brownish-pink, greenish brown
'Qat' leaves looked askance at our glazed eyes
And withdrew shyly into their plastic shells
Like demure Indian brides.

This gentle host, satisfied with all religious
Rituals, closed the door, drew the drapes,
Occupied the central seat like a priest, nodded,
And allowed us to attack the maiden leaves.

Yet, one more ritual remained unperformed!

Yes, now we poured hot, steaming Qishr
Into our chalices and lighted our king-size Rothmans.

We sipped and puffed!
Puffed and sipped—and so we began.

The attack began in unison.
We snapped the velvety soft coy leaves
From their parental stalks
And stuffed them unabashedly into our waiting mouths,
Chewing them, grinding them, sending the green nectar
Into our expectant bodies like inaudible
Music of the spheres.

The rhythm at the beginning seemed steady.
The sacred beginning gained momentum.
The cosmic speed continued unabated.

Exhausted, we now cried, "Halt."
We all chanted, "And God created 'qat'."

Notes: The tender leaves of 'qat' plant which is typical to Yemen are chewed by Yemenis almost regularly and are considered a stimulant.

The Man Who Played Lute upon Chewing 'Qat'
(Dedicated to Yahya Annono)

The divine lute he pressed close to his sacred chest;
His beaming noble heart strummed;
His joyous fingers danced on the strings;
His playful lips played the holy tune;
His gleeful head swayed like a *qat* plant in gentle breeze.

And the nylon drapes swung sideways!

The words sounded exotic;
The magical sounds turned the dark *mufraj* bright.

The head and the heart
The fingers and the strings
The lips and the sounds
Gathered all together
At the altar of music!

It was sight of soul in action!

Notes: 'Mufraj' is the typical Yemeni living room with pillows leaning against the walls for people to sit down and enjoy their parties, typically their pastime of qat-chewing sessions.

An Expedition on Ramadan Evening

The shy yellow moon's face
Hid behind the grey veil,
As four of us raced,
Raced through the narrow, rugged lane
To the remote, unkempt bare store.

The sturdy storekeeper
Craned from man-sized hole
And parted with three pink plastic sacks
Of virgin 'qat' leaves pure.

The beaming three men
Carried each of the tender sacks
As they would their brides, jumped into the car
And rushed toward the dark portal.

Upon our return, I glanced
At the naked full moon entrenched.
The 'qat' honey yet unreleased
And the coy moon embraced.

"The celestial bodies do bless our earthly spirits!"

Trip into the Past: A Visit to Rila Monastery, Bulgaria

The turn to the right on the ascending highway
From Blagoevgrad to Sofia abruptly shows the way
As the recently installed tall white Ivan Rilski's
Statue stretches its arm, points the road to holiness of the past;
We hurriedly jerk, swing, and head toward our destination.

The winding, turning, curving, narrow two-lane
Road passing through sleepy towns hugged by
Dust-coated immobilized cars, lazy nondescript dogs, alert vendors,
Unhurried bicyclists mutely showed us the way still shrouded
In mystery as we rushed to tear its encrusted veil.

The tall birches, pines; the murmuring creek; the ancient
Silent solid granite towering mountainous sides; the inter-
Weaving of the stretched arms of the trees from both sides;
The occasional blue patches of the distant sky deepened further
Our spiritual curiosity,
Our minds wandered and clashed.

Lo, behold, suddenly almost in the middle stood
A gigantic structure that dwarfed us all. A spiritual
Silence now enveloped us—nature evidently was kind
To the great being to order him to build a monastery
That would stand the test of endless time, the onslaught of invaders.

The archway sent signals to us to move in, tread the
Smooth, time-worn, weather-beaten, hard rock slabs.
And as we trepiditiously entered the Church of the
Nativity of the Virgin, the Central Monastery Church,
We all experienced a certain tranquility: peace and spirit
entombed.

The Memorable Blagoevgrad Rain

Those summer afternoon Balkan dark clouds
From Macedonia, Kosovo, Serbia
Rushed toward the serene, majestic mountains
Of Blagoevgrad and burst unabashedly
Releasing monsoon-like columns of water.

We took shelter in my Spartan office;
Managed to find solace in Rakia.
And we—the unholy trinity of anthropology,
Finance, and literature—swung with each sip
Between sacred and profane poems.

It was a plot we engineered to ignore
The elements and be our natural selves.

Blagoevgrad's Bouncing Young Women

Aha! These cream-skinned, dark, shiny wandering tresses.
High-cheek boned, push their tall frames
Shooting their glinting brown eyes and chiseled
Noses piercingly, searchingly, and sensually.
And they walk in beauty!

Wow! Their bony frames support their dark tresses
Like those trellises all over Blagoevgrad, coquettishly
Inviting the creeping grapevines.
And they meander and curl up in beauty!

Whoosh! Their small breasts like southern Bulgarian apples
Firmly concealed under orange tee shirts and green
turtlenecks
Push the ravenous onlookers toward their prancing,
Hopping, and bouncing bodies!
And they walk in beauty!

Now such a spectacle triggers in me a spark to ignite
Those erotic thoughts that keep body and soul together,
Discarding my mind for its irrational reasoning.

And I love to imagine leisurely all those prancing
Young women surrounding me like the romantic Lord
Krishna besieged by the young gopis.

Notes: Lord Krishna is famed to have been surrounded by
admiring young women known as 'gopis'.

On Rereading Tao Ch'ien

Sitting in my sacred kitchen,
I look at the window
And see the bare trees draped
In snow that seem like marble statues.

My apartment lies beside a well-traveled road;
Yet I hear no noise of passing cars.
I am content with my self-imposed solitude
And relaxing meditation.
In my old age I reread the ancient
Chinese poetry and contemplate on life and death.

I drink my Merlot alone and savor with gusto;
Its warmth keeps my spirits high and engaged.
I sit at my kitchen table and watch the world-
Chirping birds, snowy mountains, deep blue sky.

In the Company of the Ancient Chinese Poet Li Po

I don't eat mutton or sliced beef,
The ones you crave for with your wine.
But your company still makes my
Wine taste better and drives away my sorrows.
It's the company that matters, Li Po.
Together we will be spirited and joyous.

On Teaching Ancient Chinese Literature to Western Students

The short lyrical ancient Chinese poems
Imbued with the philosophy of Taoism and Confucianism
Thrill my students in America and Bulgaria
And keep their eyes sparkle and minds dazzle.

Parting

When clouds gather,
They dump rain or snow,
Based on the season or the elevation.
Sometimes they just pass by
Like travelers on freeways.
Then, they disintegrate and disappear.

When friends gather,
They share ecstasy or agony,
Depending on the season or the occasion.
Sometimes they just reminisce
Like stranded travelers at bus stations.
Then they part with a nebulous promise.

Past, Present, and Future

Past is a memory
Disjointed, fragmented;
Present is flowing
Like an unimpeded stream.
Future is yet to be shaped—
May be colored with hope.
Our thoughts only relate
To past, present, and future—
All in one instance.
So, our hope is rounded up
In ungraspable time—beaten
With the tide of time.

Watching Humming Birds

Fluttering their sparkling silvery wings,
They gather at the water trough
Suspended on a bent tree branch—
Dip their long thirsty beaks;
Sip a droplet of stale water,
Hover around, fly back swiftly—
Their dance is a sight to behold—
A divine gyration – mystical as a Sufi dance—
Is there a design in that performance!
Surely, they rest at night!
But my aged heart beats unseen
Doesn't rest – a mystical force—
Thump, thump, it beats on tirelessly
With no rest—until the last day.

Watching My Daughter Neela Perform Bharata Natyam, South Indian Classical Dance

Decked in resplendent bharata natyam blue costume and shining jewelry, She steps on to the glittering stage in measured steps, anklet bells chiming Sonorously, puts her palms together, bows before Nataraja's bronze image, To invoke the blessings of the King of Celestial Dance to perform without Missteps in unison with South Indian classical dance music, imbued with ardor,
She begins to glide like a swan with complex footwork in motion like peacock
Spread, hops continually, glistening eye gestures rhythmically, a symphony of feet, eyes, hands, to narrate Lord Krishna's love song passionately translating
The story in ballet, drama, and myth synthesis in graceful gyration all over.
The sparkling stage—a consummation that fulfills the intended performance.
A scintillating life force in action! A kaleidoscopic feast it is!
The spectators' eyes sparkle in solemnity enchanted by the buffet.

On Growing Old!

I grow old wrapped in the shawl of fears!
I grow old trapped in the shell of cares!
I grow old caged behind bars of medicines!
I grow old stupefied by hearing aids!

When I was a youth, I was uncouth!
Being old now, I have lost warmth!
All is not lost; my spirit keeps me cheerful
And grounded to face fears and terror.

Modern Old Age

Modern old age promises
Uncertain fragile longevity
With television commercials
That cage me in dentures, bladder control pills,
Ever-changing high tech hearing aids,
'life-alert' necklaces, painless cataract surgeries,
Comfortable assisted living,
To burden me more with wants—
Driving me crazy with blaring ads
For 'hover around' to make me immobile.

But I silently escape into my sanctuary
Of glorious reading and pious meditation.

My ninety-six-year-old father in India
Passed away gently, untouched by any

My Sacred Body

My sacred body—the
Abode of my Holy Trinity—
My spirit, mind, and body—
Is enriched daily by prayers,
Ennobled by silent meditation,
Nourished by reading and writing,
And fed with healthy nutrients—
Is what I value and respect most.

I Stand Tall

I stand erect and tall,
So I won't droop and fall.
I hear a wild call
That comes from afar,
Or, from within near,
So, my inward fear
Won't crumple and tear me

Wither My Mother Tongue, Telugu!!!

I am starved for my mother tongue, Telugu, drying up drip by drip' I am distressed there is no one in this small town who speaks Telugu. My proficiency shriveled up over two decades, more so after divorce. It's a language rich with fifty-two consonants and twelve vowels, each in letters that has facilitated me to pronounce and enunciate other languages such as Russian, Bulgarian, Romanian, French, Czech, English. Now, impoverished for want of nourishment, my mother tongue has deserted me like a Chinese panda without bamboo shoots.

More than four decades ago I uprooted myself from my native soil, India, and re-rooted in the fertile American soil enriched with nutrients. I stand out by being brown, so do my children born in America; neither I nor my children don't want to be yelled at thoughtlessly by ignorant racists—"go back to where you belong". *We belong here.*

Communion*

Inside Moorty's cupboard, a picture of God
is waiting. You reach for the Post Toasties
and God watches you, even when you
retreat all the way to the table and bow –
even if you close the door of course
you can't escape. Moorty knows that,
and you do too. Thank you, Moorty,
and thank you God – and for the Post Toasties.

At the table talk ranges – Australia,
life in England, following The Virgin
River. A woman from next door carries
her own wine in, already opened,
and pours it around in the beer mugs.
Everything begins to get sacred. I will remember
Moorty, and Australia, the bell in the short-wave
oven, and what is inside any cupboard.

30 July 1988   William Stafford
                                United States Poet Laureate 1970

(*Note: In the United States, as in India, most Hindu homes
either have a separate altar room with pictures of the gods for
worship or, lacking room, accommodate the pictures inside a
section of the kitchen cupboard, which then serves as an altar
for daily worship.)

Stories

Grandpa! Where Is He?

(Translated from Telugu, a Dravidian language of South India – considered the Italian of the East)

"How long! How many more years? Oh! Grandpa is ageing – becoming very, very old day by day!"

"My son was born in the U.S. to parents of Indian origin and doesn't have any preconditioned eating habits, no desire to have Indian curry or spicy food!

Quite happily he would tackle hamburgers, pizza, pasta, and eat with gusto and relish! He has never been to India. He is now twenty-three. He even dates American girls. But he has never been to India."

Even in scouting he excelled. He earned his Eagle Scout Award at the age of fifteen. To top it, he went to Australia to attend the World Scout Jamboree – he came back sick as though the gods didn't want to shower their blessings on a grandson who hasn't seen his grandpa. He has never visited India. He hasn't seen his grandpa – his dad's dad. His grandma passed away a couple of years ago. This grandson hasn't seen his grandparents!

***

"Grandpa is ninety-six. Granted! During this December break the grandson could fly to India for a couple of weeks and connect with his grandpa," thus his dad ruminated continually. "Very expensive to send grandson! Yet, family connections are vital. And, dad isn't an engineer; neither is he a medical doctor, nor is he a computer scientist. He has very limited financial resources. To top it, dad's wife is extravagant with her spend-thriftiness. She had driven dad into tight financial comers."

"Now, how long will grandpa live?"

It's really exciting to go to India – the ancient land – for the first time. If the young grandson were to go to India in summer, then possibly he might hate India – to experience the unbearable tropical heat, to bear miseries with inconveniences with travel in India, the masses, the confusion, the chaos; the grandson doesn't know any of the languages, perhaps finding difficult to handle hot food that cousins may shower on him as 'treat'; yes, he will be inundated with lots of love like those monsoon rains that flood vast areas of India. 'Perhaps going during December vacation will be much better,' thought dad.

* * *

Grandson doesn't seem to demonstrate any particular desire to visit India. Grandson's dad is, however, becoming anxious day by day – time is running out – somehow or other, dad has been planning to send his son to grandpa. In that continual planning, reflection, agitation, dad ruminated: "America, India – two huge countries, two democracies; one is a natural mother, the other an adopted mother; the one is an old, ancient country; the other is a new, rich country." All these political, philosophical thoughts were engaging dad.

The young son wasn't caught in the web of uncertainties, agitation. It was all in his dad's mind – his conflict. To his son, India presented simply itself as an idea. Just an amorphous idea – not an emotional attachment! Yet out of love for his dad, out of respect for his dad, the son thought about his dad's country of origin – the birthplace – and eventually about his grandpa. Yes, he did look at his grandpa's picture a few times. But it was just a picture, a photo – no connection to the real, living grandfather. He never saw the flesh-and-blood grandpa!

The local American friends inquired of the young fellow. From Indian letters from dad's father, from dad's sisters, from dad's brothers, and kith and kin started flooding dad's home.

178

And dad's friends from around the world would inquire, "Has your son even been to India?" "Don't you want your son to see his grandpa?" "And you lost your mother a couple of years ago!" "And your father is close to being a centenarian!" "You have to send your son to India!"

***

Eventually the son started showing some interest in visiting India – the land of his father, his grandfather, and all the ancestors. "Yes, dad, I really want to visit India; I desperately want to see my grandpa. It was unfortunate that I didn't get a chance to see my grandma, your oldest brother, my uncle. I believe my grandpa is close to one hundred years. I have made up my mind. I will visit grandpa this coming December." Then the grandson began to experience new thoughts, new respect, new emotions, and an inexplicable affection. He even entertained a new respect toward Alex Halley. We all saw the famous mini-series 'Roots' in late 1970s. In fact, Alex Halley came to our small town. I believe it was in 1980s.

We all attended his lecture. Later, we met him. We even had his autograph on our copy of Roots.

***

Now 1996.

In February, one early morning our phone range ominously – rather unusual for that hour. Dad was in bed – he liked to sleep in on Saturdays. Dad's brother's son in New Jersey was on the other end.

"Uncle, I received a call from Hyderabad that grandpa passed away."

***

It was sudden, though grandpa was close to one hundred. Dad was quiet. He showed his emotions in his solemn grief.

His son recognized it. Both dad and son embraced. "I am sorry dad that you have lost your dad. But I have lost my grandpa. And I have lost my unvisited India of my grandpa. I will certainly visit India." Teardrops trickled down grandson's cheeks. Dad wiped them.

(I originally wrote this in Telugu; the story was published in Telugu Paluku, the bilingual souvenir publication of the 11th TANA Convention, July 1997 Anaheim Convention Center, California)

P.S.: 2018: Now my son is forty-five, married to an Andhra girl, Telugu – speaking, an Indian American. They have a seven-year-old son. All of them have visited India twice. Now my son enjoys Andhra dishes such as pesarattu and pacchhadis.

The Homecoming

Exhausted, he came back home—that tiny town of thirteen families at the foot of the rugged mountains in the Lewis-Clark national forest in Montana—dragging his feet in the mounds of snow. He thought he deserved an emotional welcome hug and a shower of kisses from his wife. It was certainly homecoming to Adam Herculitius, not just a mere homecoming to one who has been away for one, two, three, or ten years. Adam had been given up as lost in time and space. Dead! There could be no homecoming for one who was considered dead, except as an airy, floating spirit!

He returned to his home in that cold, foggy, dark, and pitiless evening like a shadowy shapeless figure from that country unknown to living human beings.

For the first month when Adam disappeared, he was considered lost by his wife, Eva, his two sons, the thirteen-year-old Ken and the eleven-year-old Eble, by his independent-loving neighbors, and by the seven—member search party. Those thirty-one days of January moved heavily between anxiety and eagerness, between expectation and despair. Particularly Eva thought she felt so. The surrounding snowcovered solid mountains threatened Eva's lingering hopes that started slowly receding into the inaccessible trail-less sections of the snow. Her conscience turned hazy and fragmented like the distant boulders at the far end of the stream – one that skirted around the town gently in summer – that no more moved, frozen solid without emotions with a blank, deathly stare. Eva's brown, furry dog now looked like a wild animal of tropical forests. Adam's color picture that sat on the fireplace mantle in the living-room assumed remoteness, lifelessness, perhaps just a fading memory of a certain time of the past that was momentarily frozen and stilled – a memory of the mind, a living being of the past.

The tossing moments of Eva's confused conscience of January drifted into a vague acquiescence of her new status of being without her husband by the beginning of February. She spent most of the twenty-eight days of February adjusting to a new-dawn independence and sorting out the possible financial windfall that might flood her with one hundred thousand dollars, moving to Great Falls, Montana, living in a posh and plush newly built condominium, instead of continuing to exist in the ramshackle, rickety thirty-three-year-old house of peeling paint, cracking doors, leaking faucets. 'After all, life has to be lived, not tolerated,' rationalized Eva. 'I have to live my life.'

Her piled-up emotions of loss resulting in a twisted life of grief and sorrow froze up – metamorphosed into a rock. Now it is a thing of the past. She refused to be buried in the debris of her present listless life. New ideas started springing in her, almost making her neighbors feel uneasy with her passionate desire to overcome grief. They even suspected that perhaps she had looked forward to such a natural situation to develop so she could do what she had wanted from the beginning of her moving into that remote, small, vague, anonymous town.

The search party's confirmation that Adam certainly had perished – no one really questioned the need for solid proof or tangible evidence – during the mighty blizzard that battered the town immediately after Christmas, gave birth in Eva a strong will to explore means of finding all possible financial resources for the present and future. It was then she vigorously confronted her own self and questioned her hidden soul; she thought it was tucked away somewhere in her being, though she didn't see it.

'After all, it is the society that goads me to love my husband; why should I if he isn't anymore? Why love and cherish something that doesn't exist? I love myself. I am alive and full of life. The society doesn't care one way or the other. My neighbors look at me from outside. But I'm the only one that is capable of looking at myself inwards. The society doesn't feed me, doesn't care about my wishes, my life, my concerns. The society comes up with only empty words of sympathy. That is all! I may be considered strange, weird, callous, inhuman, for not having observed my due respect for the dead, Adam, for not having completed emotional search. Why should I? Why should I?'

Her inner self started raising its ugly head like an untamed bear searching for its prey. She had suppressed it for long.

'Since I haven't seen the remains of Adam, it's possible he may return in a strange shape. Or, even if he comes back, why should I now accept him?'

It was toward the end of February that she finally resolved not to think of Adam anymore?

'Why think of something that doesn't really exist in the house? Well, Ken and Eble need to be taken care of. After all, they've grudgingly and vaguely accepted Adam's death.'

By the first week of March, the prudent insurance agent had already assured Eva of a fat check by the time she moved into condominium in Great Falls. The omnipotent money will be her new husband, her security, her strength, her success, her society, and the new father to the boys. After all, what more does one want in this world? She finally decided to erase her fifteen-year-old marriage with Adam in a fleeting moment of robust decision immediately after the agent left her doorstep on that Friday morning.

Despite her newborn strength of mind, Eva couldn't sleep for the rest of the seven nights she was to spend in that eerie house and the snow-covered town. Adam, the corner-street gas station, the neighbors, the frozen stream, and the dark, tall, ghostly mountains, still haunted her; her living thoughts entwined in those that made no sense to her life. Nights crept slowly but remained longer, tiresome. For protection, she would let Ken and Eble sleep beside her. No amount of firmness or strength of mind eased her nagging thoughts.

It was the last night she was to sleep in that house of terror and memory. The previous two days brought more snow, more howling wind, more frequent power failures, more isolation from neighbors, and more appetite.

Feeling hungry and realizing no food in the refrigerator, Eva slowly, holding a flickering candle, stumbled toward the freezer to pick up the last piece of raw venison that Adam had stacked up during the hunting season in October. As she lifted the freezer door and tumbled for that chunk, she heard faint steps at the hack of the kitchen. Half-ignoring those un-earthly sounds, Eva holding her cold venison, fleetingly darted her glance, still suspicious of Adam's lingering being. When she confronted a grizzly, phantomlike huge figure of Adam beckoning her from behind the glass door, the door that thinly separates the house and the rest of the world of figures, of people, of darkness, of snow, using discretion more than emotion, she suppressed her scream and her shock. Dictated more by instinct, she sprinted into her bedroom. Quickly, she returned with Adam's handgun and pointing toward Adam's figure, Eva said gently, "Even if you're really alive, I want you to be dead now. Why do you deal a deathblow to those that are alive? I want to live. You were dead. Be dead now. Be gone. Let no one know... Don't you want Ken and Eble to be prosperous with all the money I will get soon from your death?"

The words were like bullets to Adam. From out of the darkness that stretched endlessly and beyond the mountains, he came to the light of his home. Now, he left the house and went into his new home of mountains, muttering, "Oh! Eva, evil Eva, have I lived painfully so far only to see you dead?"

The River Of Return

More than two decades ago! Early fall! Saturday morning! Krishna banged the front door, shaking the foundation of his dream house in the Halladay neighborhood of Salt Lake City, Utah, rushed to the carport, kicked the rear of his 1977 VW Rabbit, flung open the driver's side door, plopped on the black vinyl seat, turned the ignition, jerkily reversed the car, joined the quiet residential street, headed toward the 5th south exit, and let the steering wheel decide his choking mind. It was soon after a heated squabble with his wife which he couldn't squelch. Being a quiet and withdrawing type, he left the house to sort out his disturbed mind. He drove aimlessly toward Craig, Montana—somehow the name had an obsessive appeal to him. He liked the drive on I-15 North from Salt Lake City to Lethbridge, Alberta, Canada. Craig is just a small nondescript town sitting alongside the Missouri river that jig-jagged and meandered hugged by tall pine trees. He thought his life seemed purposeless. He felt he had nothing to live for. It was his sudden realization that drove him uncontrollably away from his moorings in Salt Lake City. Probably something in him goaded him behind the steering wheel and let the wheels run the course. He has let his life run its full course? How could that be? He was just a robust thirty-seven. Or, was he going to renounce his material and physical self? Surely, no one could fathom the depths of his troubled mind!

Krishna himself didn't know.

The winding Missouri river's majestic flow and its placid shimmering waters profoundly moved toward its appointed destination that attracted Krishna's tired and undirected attention. The unnoticeable exist at Craig somehow fatalistically pulled Krishna to slow down.

Krishna parked screechingly, his Rabbit near the sloping left bank of the river. Yes, one can brake one's car suddenly, but can one stop the rhythm of life abruptly and awkwardly? Krishna vaguely concluded as though he had spent all the time except for a pit stop for gas and McDonald's quarter pounder and coke in his dark brown Rabbit—he drove for nearly thirteen hours, though he didn't seem to be conscious of it when he did.

He didn't care whether or not he should slam shut the car's door. He left the door open—'closing the door would mean,' he thought, 'shutting the doors of perception of life and death, of heaven and hell, of love and jealousy.' He just didn't bother; in fact, he didn't bother about the trivia in his life. And what he cared for, craved for, and sought after incessantly and assiduously, he believed, was never respected nor understood by his own immediate family—his wife, Rukku, and his seven-year-old son, Balu. Rukku didn't even bother to understand Krishna—it was an arranged marriage—for she was too busy with her own life, her crafts projects, her dreams, and her social activities and engagements. This was how Krishna rationalized.

Krishna led a tempestuous life inwardly as long as he was with Rukku. Except for the short romantic spell during their honeymoon in Kodaikanal, Krishna could hardly recall anything tender, warm, and touching from Rukku except her wifely duties in the bedroom. Once again, Krishna indulged in his inimitable fashion of generalizing and rationalizing the superficially observed gestures and hints. Perhaps romantic spells need only be remembered in a dreamlike fashion. And courting is the time when you conceal the most and reveal the least, whereas reality is a painful revelation of your weaknesses and limitations. Being sensitive and sharp, Krishna never cared to verify with Rukku her attitudes and concerns toward him. For some time, he philosophized that it was a feminine quality for an Indian wife to conceal her feelings and affections toward her husband unlike the American style demonstration of affection. At times, he even fantasized the romantic American or the western-style dating. He thought there was excitement in that!

Rukku continued with her life pattern of shopping—going to ZCMI, K Mart, going to shopping malls, watching daytime dramas, playing tennis, and social drinking. What she cared for was herself and routinely taking care of Balu. Since Krishna neither yelled at nor threw dinner plates in the kitchen, Rukku at no stage even thought of anything amiss between her and Krishna. And to the neighborhood and the community, Krishna and Rukku presented a shining and model picture of matrimonial bliss. Actually there seemed no conflict, no disharmony, and no disagreement on anything serious. This is how I as their neighbor perceived.

Outwardly, there seemed no marital problem. We, the neighbors, began to recognize the validity of arranged marriages. Anyway, as later Krishna admitted, it was all in Krishna's mind. How could Rukku divine that Krishna was anguished! Krishna never complained; he never whimpered; he never quarreled; he never made any demands on Rukku. Krishna never objected to the master-charge bills that simply mounted because of Rukku's compulsive and senseless buying. Rukku, who came from a background of total parental control, found out that she could have hair down after marriage. But Krishna suffered stoically and silently the pain that Rukku, without her knowledge, without being conscious, inflicted on him.

Now Krishna was away from the unbearable troublesome atmosphere of his family. For the first time in the nine years of his married life, he has forgotten all the teasing and tortuous problems of his life. He forgot, temporarily though, the issues that made him leave abruptly his home in Salt Lake City. Why did he have to leave his precious belongings, his love and family, and all the material wealth that he amassed in his profession as an anesthesiologist with the LDS hospital? Why did he have to seek refuge on the banks of Missouri? It's unusual—almost a sin—for a medical practitioner to seek knowledge in and understanding of fine arts, religion, and philosophy. Krishna is unique among Indian medical doctors.

His insatiable thirst for knowledge often times led him to question life, living, life after death, the life of Buddha, and the life of Hindu sage. Once after watching the movie 'Siddhartha', because of his *Bollywood* favorite actor Shashi Kapoor being in the lead role, he devoured Herman Hesse's novel. His present contemplative postures on the banks of Missouri may obliquely suggest that he was pursuing the life pattern of Siddhartha. Maybe Krishna was in pursuit of something spiritual; maybe he was seeking answers to some unanswered questions in his life. It looked like Krishna was oblivious to the fact that had a wife, a son, and that Rukku was carrying his baby.

What he was conscious of was that he was on the banks of the Missouri River, a river that is gentle, deep, and serene— almost reflecting *nirvanic* calmness, a river that is alive and animated by an invisible force in as much as a man's life is animated by a supernatural force, a river that has been flowing since the beginning of time, beyond easily measurable time, a river that has silently observed the mutations of the humans, a river that has quenched the thirst of the parched throats of humans, animals, and farms alike.

The glitter of the waters dazzled Krishna. He looked piercingly at the cloudless immense blue sky and immediately bent down and penetratingly and thoughtfully looked at the slow-moving waters—there is certainly life in the gentle vibrations like the kicking of baby in its mother's womb.

'What is this stuff 'love' made of?' mused Krishna. Surely he felt marriage as such did not perpetuate love. Love is like a firecracker that illumines the dark blue sky in all its splendor and variegated colors followed by a deafening sound. Is it all sound with no substance? Krishna felt cheated. He calculated that it was Rukku who immensely gained out of their marriage. If love demands sacrifice, then sacrifice on whose part? At least from Krishna's point of view, it was a total sacrifice. He sacrificed his independence, his time, his energy, his tastes, his desires, and his hobbies. For Rukku's sake, he magnanimously controlled his voracious reading; for her sake, he curtailed his visits to concerts, ballets, and plays. And what did Rukku do or sacrifice for Krishna's sake? Krishna couldn't think of anything particular or specific. Just a vague feeling! But Rukku didn't even suggest that he ought to give up anything Krishna prized or valued.

Sitting meditatively, Krishna could recall distinctly one incident between him and Rukku early in their marriage. After three glorious months of marriage during which time both Krishna and Rukku talked incessantly of their premarital romantic days, on a tiresome fall Friday afternoon, Krishna returned home from the hospital rather early. Though Rukku was surprised, she didn't enquire why Krishna had returned early. Krishna expected a sense of tender care, warmth, concern, and sympathy from Rukku. To Rukku, it was a little upsetting because she had already planned out her tennis practice with her coach, Jim Stringfellow.

"Darling, you're home early today," casually enquired Rukku. "Rukku, you seem to be all set for tennis. Do you think you can skip today's practice?" Krishna quipped in a plaintive and suggestive tone.

There was no further exchange. Rukku didn't feel anything wrong with Krishna, except that he was back home unusually before his normal expected time. So she left home in a casual and sweeping manner, leaving Balu to the care of Krishna. This set Krishna thinking. 'Could there be an affair between Jim and Rukku?' Krishna vaguely surmised. 'No. No, there can't be.' What disturbed Krishna was Rukku's nonchalance. Since then, Rukku and her attitude remained an enigma to Krishna. It was a philosophical question that had no easy answer. He would simply question within himself, 'Why? Why…' He made no determined effort to confront Rukku, no prying on the privacy of Rukku, nor did he verify his suspicions. But certainly the incident converted the introvert Krishna into a suspicious husband. He knew suspicion would breed ill will. He remembered his grandmother's famous Telugu proverb that 'suspicion is an overpowering ghost that lurks forever.' Without ever expressing, Krishna began to detach himself from Rukku;

Rukku didn't suspect any indifference or coldness—she was engrossed in her own activities and wifely duties.

Krishna sat motionless like a solid rock close to Missouri. No one could say what thoughts passed through in his tortured mind. Maybe he contemplated suicide; maybe he decided to leave the family for good. Maybe he wanted to try with Rukku for the sake of family unity and for Balu's future. Maybe he wanted to probe the whole matter. But what is there to probe? Ultimately he decided to go back home.

Krishna grabbed a ham sandwich from a nearby restaurant. It was the first sign of his coming back to reality of life. It occurred to him then that after all, he was never denied food at home. Rukku loved to cook all varieties of ethnic foods, including Krishna's favorite South Indian dishes. Krishna didn't have to make frequent trips to *Pizza Hut*. Rukku took care of it. And love was not denied either.

Back again on the road with determination and a desire to talk to Rukku, now there was a destination—home.

It was past midnight when he reached his home. The carport was fully lit, ablaze. The front door to the house was wide open. There was Jim Stringfellow's blue Dodge on the driveway. In the living room could be seen Rukku and Jim. Rukku seemed to be lost if her blank stare was any indication; Jim was thumbing through Time Magazine. The little Balu was in his pajamas with his head on Rukku's lap. Krishna could detect a deep sense of concern and anguish in the whole atmosphere.

Krishna entered the living room trepiditiously; even then, the soft sounds suddenly awakened Rukku as if from a disturbing dream. Rukku jumped from lazy-boy and rushed like a flash flood toward Krishna. "Jim... Jim... Krishna is back," yelled Rukku full-throatedly. The sounds reverberated through the whole house. There was a happy harmony of lights, sounds, and sights.

Before Krishna could suspect any further, Rukku kissed Krishna longingly and passionately on his dry lips. Detaching her wet lips painfully, Rukku asked Krishna to meet Jim.

"Krishna, you know, Jim has all along been trying to console me. He is not only my tennis coach, my friend Laura's husband, but has been like a brother."

Shaken and troubled but enlightened, Krishna gasped: "My gosh! Am I glad I didn't go off the deep...? It was the river!"

When Krishna recounted and narrated succinctly after a week, I, his neighbor of three years, felt and imaginatively experienced the cultural difference between America and India. In fact, I was even transported back to my undergraduate years at UCLA when in my literature classes I was exposed to Walt Whitman's 'Passage to India' and E.M. Forster's novel 'A Passage to India'.

Temple Bells

It was his routine, a routine that he religiously performed for seven years. And all he longed for was advancement in his job and enough money to take care of his wife.

When the distant temple bells would toll precisely at seven o'clock every evening, Ramu would rush from his one-room abode – actually an outhouse adjoining the local money – lender's house – wash his hands, and sprint toward the far end of the street, bearing with him his uneasy load of injustice of life. And the bells would continue to toll until he almost reached the sacred plot of the temple.

Seven years of worship – a kind of mechanical chore – has not fructified in any tangible rewards. Yet his trust in the magical and mystical powers of the supernatural deities had not deserted him. He believed blindly.

As soon as he reached the holy spot that muggy and rainy Friday evening, the sweltering end of June, he, as usual, circumambulated the temple thrice, gently stepped inside and rang the brass bells, folded his hands in deference to the mightiness of the stony idol, bowed as a sign of his insignificance before the immutable Unknown, and eventually prostrated before the dark, oily image. The shirtless Brahmin priest lighted camphor on a shiny copper plate and moved it hurriedly thrice clockwise while confusingly invoking the blessings of the Divine in an incomprehensible language. He carefully picked a few marigolds and green fragrant leaves and placed in the cupped hands of Ramu. With a copper spoon, the priest dropped a few drops of sanctified water in the devotee's carefully adjusted hands. Ramu sipped the water.

Such a glorious ritual! Similarly Ramu performed his duties as a lower division clerk in the state government office devoted to tax levy and collection for fourteen years. In his office, his superiors were almost like gods. Those changing gods at least blatantly demonstrated their anger or petty indifference but never their satisfaction with Ramu's diligence and efficiency. He felt his colleagues with 'connections' were promoted or their sloppy work was never questioned. What about the real gods? "Can I have connections with gods?" Ramu would muse periodically.

Ramu brought back in his folded hands a piece of fresh coconut the priest offered to share with his wife, Rukku, hoping that the gods would bless her with a child.

They have been married for about fourteen years – The first seven years were a mere span of marital ecstasy and comfort; the past seven years prolonged like a tropical summer afternoon. Struggle, self-torture!

"I don't trust the efficacy of these sacred coconut pieces anymore," retorted Rukku. "After all, we've performed prayers, visited holy places like Tirupati, bribed the gods and the priests, have had only dips in Ganga, Godavary, and Kauvery, fed the Brahmins, and gave donations for temples. You name it! My God, we've done every conceivable thing to please the gods above. And you've also tried to please and humor the gods in your office. Have you had any promotions? Your friend Krishna, a mere bachelor's degree holder, has even become an upper division clerk. And... and... have I conceived yet? No! Have we won any lottery or fortune? No! If there is no meaning or purpose in life, if there is no charm or pleasure, then why should we suffer to continue our daily visits to the temple? Please stop from now on."

Such perorations were a routine with Rukku.

But on that particular rainy evening, when Ramu rushed back from the temple in mud, slush, and sweat, Rukku ebulliently smiled at him – perhaps the first natural one in seven years – instead of reproaching him. Stunned and perplexed, he muttered, "What miraculous events have taken place in the past forty minutes?"

"Oh, our neighbor widow visited with me. And she quoted Lord Krishna's counsel to the warrior Arjuna from the Bhagavad Gita. 'In work thy rightful interest should lie, nor even in its fruits; let not thy motive be the fruit of work; to no work let not thine attachment be.'"

Ramu wiped his sweat in Rukku's saree.

Embrace

A small town in New Jersey (The name of this town of about four thousand people is of little consequence.)

A black owner of a corner grocery store when he arrived around 7:30 in the morning of 2nd May, having already stashed away his troubled feelings about the distant rioting, looting, shooting, and killing of south central L.A., saw to his dismay on the white wall – the space saved for posters of several small sale items – of his store bold letters staring threateningly in black: "You don't belong here. Close the store. If you don't in two days, your store will be looted."

Immediately, he opened the store and called the local police. Within half an hour, two cops – one white and the other black – rushed to the store without sirens. They looked at the graffiti and assured the owner, Henry Haley, that he shouldn't worry about such trivial things. After the cops left the scene, Henry picked up a spray paint can, went outside, and emptied the whole can to erase the graffiti.

The second day, after the first incident, Henry again noticed graffiti: "Don't waste your paint. You shut down the store."

The few regular customers, who came to buy milk, cigarettes, and beer, sympathized with Henry's plight and concern. "Henry, you've been here for more than ten years. Why do you have to put up with this? You belong here. Haven't you filed a complaint?"

The second day's graffiti troubled Henry deeply. His mind reeled back to the days of Martin Luther King, Jr., the Peace March in Washington, D. C., and the wave of racial integration. Now those days seemed a mere dream. The present nightmare hurt his sight and his soul.

As he was vaguely looking at the shelves, a white boy, Tom Sharpe, a thirteen-year-old, a regular candy customer of Henry, barged in, yelling, "Mr. Haley, where are you?" Henry materialized. "Is that you, Tom? I haven't seen you during the past two days. Have you been sick? Do you need *M&Ms*?"

Tom sheepishly nodded his head. He remained in the store longer than his usual transaction time. Henry went back to the shelves. Yet he noticed from the corner of his eye that Tom was vaguely looking at him.

"Mr. Haley, you look strange."

Henry didn't pay attention

"Mr. Haley, you know what? Are you different from me? Why are you different from white folks?"

Henry now came closer to Tom and stood close to him. "Tom, you look different today. Something is bothering you. I think you've secret that you want to share. Aren't you different from your brother Steve who, I believe, is a senior in high school?"

Tom shirked a little. "Mr. Haley, are you worried with all the graffiti on the wall?"

Henry began to see Tom raising his shoulders, avoiding eye-contact, and acting uneasy. Now suspicious of Tom's behavior, Henry paternally asked Tom: "Do you know who has been writing this graffiti on my store wall? I am your friend."

Tom, still nervous and hesitant, haltingly muttered, "Well, my friends in the middle school wanted to challenge me…"

Being almost certain, Henry picked up a quart of chocolate milk and put in Tom's cold hands and hugged him. Suddenly, Tom started crying bitterly.

"Mr. Haley, will you please… please forgive me? Will you still be my friend?"

They embraced. Henry wiped Tom's tears with white Kleenex.

A Christmas Gift!!!

Even before our Christmas break started, we argued acrimoniously for several stormy days—leave our cozy and warm home only if the massive snow storm that was raging for a week subsided and cleared up just spend the Christmas break with my wife's folks in Lethbridge, Alberta, Canada, more than a thousand miles away from Cedar City, Utah! And to drive straight on Interstate-15, due north, lasting more than two days through the snowbound states of Utah, Idaho, and Montana seemed a chilling venture and a daunting task. I grumbled: "No sane person would undertake such a threatening and burdensome adventure, especially with uncertain weather looming on the horizon."

Our six-year-old boy yelled, "Dad, it would be fun, exciting, and cool!"

Our one-year girl continued with her shrill tones, "Go! Go!"

And my wife moaned, "Why don't you like visiting my folks?" Caught between the excitement of our children and the nagging complaints of my wife, I eventually grudgingly yielded to the pressure. In fact, the previous summer we visited her folks without any reservations on my part.

Just three days before Christmas, the reluctant sun smiled on our family, after continual snowstorms that resulted in fender-benders on I-15. On 22nd December morning, finally, despite my protestations and reluctance, we trooped into our yellow Volkswagen bug. On the first day without any struggle with the weather, we made all the way to Idaho Falls by evening before sunset.

As we were checking into Motel Six, some weary customers at the registration desk, overhearing my mild complaints and reservations about road adventure and the sanity of continuing our long trip that still lay ahead, cautioned us about the snow-packed slick roads that we were to traverse.

"Why don't you travel south for Christmas? We are coming from Edmonton and Calgary and zooming toward Disneyland," quipped one of the customers at the counter. Our exuberant son didn't have any mature advice to offer, being wrapped up in his excitement of travel. My wife groaned incoherently that I was perhaps unwilling to be in the midst of her warm folks. Her mumbled thought expressed menacingly was more a stab at my frozen and helpless lone voice.

The following morning, we checked out of the motel by six o'clock, scrambled through a sizzling breakfast at a nearby *McDonalds*, and hit the Interstate in the semi-darkness of the morning made bright only by the ice-packed roads. All of us agreed that I would drive only at 25 MPH as long as the roads were glassy and slippery. No stops either for coffee or hotdogs since exits and entrances away from and to the freeway might prove to be hazardous. The sense of collective sacrifice pleased me. Yet, I was nervous and terrified at the prospect of covering the never-ending devilish stretch of road that lay ahead of us.

By late afternoon, we managed to be on dry patches of the freeway, about fifteen miles south of Great Falls, Montana. Then, at the insistence of my wife, to make up for the lost time, I decided to increase the speed to 55 MPH. Yet my wife suggested that I should change the gear for greater grip of the tires. No sooner I changed the gear than the vehicle suddenly made an S-turn. Evidently, I hit a black ice patch—and bounced on a snow-packed embankment, precipitously and dangerously hugging a nearby power pole. Just at the moment when the car gyrated, I felt as though my body was missing from the driver's seat! How lucky we were that there was no vehicle behind us! Our son thought that it was a stupendous adventure—he always liked the rides in Lagoon, near Salt Lake City, and those in *Disneyland*. My wife shrieked that we were lucky! The one-year-old baby cried for a few minutes.

Once again, I thought it was sheer stupidity to have ventured out on our odyssey in the wrong season of the year in a wrong direction! Wow! Not a scratch on us! A flat tire! Cold winds blasted us as we nervously stepped out of the car! Gray darkness began to descend on us!

Now, after we disgorged, though shaken, out of the disabled vehicle and nervously stood by it, with cold winds blasting our faces, we saw a highway patrol car with lights flashing come into our view which evidently was coming toward us. The two cops enquired about the accident and started on fixing the flat tire with the spare tire. Right at that very moment, another passing vehicle evidently hit the same black ice spot and uncontrollably swung in our direction. In utter desperation, we immediately rolled down the embankment with the one-year-old in my arms. Shaken by the second accident that now totaled my car, helplessness enveloped us as to how our remaining journey would end. The cops recommended that we all get into their warm vehicle with the promise that they would drop us off at Best Western Motel in Great Falls, Montana, to recoup, rest, and recover from the accidents we had so agonizingly experienced. We survived the double accident just a day before Christmas. That was our Christmas gift to us all.

OM OM OM
Gayatri Maha Mantra (Chanting – Jaap)

Aum Bhur Bhuvah Svaha
Tat Savitur Varenyum
Bhargo Devasya Dheemahi
Dhiyo Yo Nah Prachodayat

Two English renditions of the above Sanskrit sloka:

1) O! omnipresent God! Keep us away from evil intentions and physical sufferings. O! Divine Enlightener and creator of the universe, lead us to Light, and direct our intellect to virtuous paths for attaining ultimate emancipation.
2) O! effulgent light that has given birth to all spheres of consciousness, O God! Who appears through the shining sun, illumine our intellect.